All About Ground Covers

Created and designed by
the editorial staff of
ORTHO BOOKS

Editor
Nancy Arbuckle

Writers
Monica Brandies
Don Dimond
Michael MacCaskey

Designer
Gary Hespenheide

Ortho Books

Publisher
Robert B. Loperena

Editorial Director
Christine Jordan

Production Director
Ernie S. Tasaki

Managing Editors
Robert J. Beckstrom
Michael D. Smith
Sally W. Smith

System Manager
Linda M. Bouchard

Editorial Assistants
Joni Christiansen
Sally J. French

Address all inquiries to:
Ortho Books
Box 5047
San Ramon, CA 94583

Copyright © 1982, 1993
Monsanto Company
All rights reserved under international and Pan-American copyright conventions.

4 5 6 7 8 9
98

ISBN 0-89721-254-1
Library of Congress Catalog Card Number 92-61735

THE SOLARIS GROUP
6001 Bollinger Canyon Road
San Ramon, CA 94583

Acknowledgments

Photography Editor
Judy Mason

Illustrator
Andrea Tachiera

Copyeditor
Barbara Feller-Roth

Indexer
Elinor Lindheimer

Layout by
Cynthia Putnam

Editorial Coordinator
Cass Dempsey

Proofreaders
Alicia K. Eckley
David Sweet

Composition by
Laurie A. Steele

Production by
Indigo Design & Imaging

Separations by
Color Tech Corp.

Lithographed in the USA by
Webcrafters, Inc.

Consultant
Michael Dirr, University of Georgia; Athens, Geor.

Special Thanks to
American Ivy Society, Mt. Vernon, Virg.
Calloway Gardens, Pine Mountain, Geor.
Canadian Department of Agricultural Research, Research Station, Summerland, British Columbia
Classic Ground Covers, Athens, Geor.
J. W. Couperthwaite, Dallas Nurseries Garden Center, Dallas, Tex.
Cunningham Gardens, Waldron, Ind.
Raymond T. Entenmann, Lambert Landscape Co., Dallas, Tex.
Morgan "Bill" Evans, landscape architect, Malibu, Calif.
Barbara Fealy, landscape architect, Beaverton, Ore.
Catherine Habiger, Menlo Park, Calif.
Allen C. Haskell, New Bedford, Mass.
Edith Henderson, landscape architect, Atlanta, Geor.
Carl McCord, Landscape Design & Construction Co., Dallas, Tex.
McDonald's Nursery, Walnut Creek, Calif.
Bridget Makk, Menlo Park, Calif.
Mannings Heather Farm, Sebastopol, Calif.
Monrovia Nursery Co., Azusa, Calif.
Mountain View Nursery, Calgary, Alberta
Kay O'Neill, Menlo Park, Calif.
Planting Fields Arboretum, Oyster Bay, Long Island, N.Y.
Rancho Santa Ana Botanic Garden, Claremont, Calif.
Royal Botanical Garden, Hamilton, Ontario
Fritz Schaeffer, Atlantic Nurseries, Long Island, N.Y.
Sidney Shore, TORO, Minneapolis, Minn.
Robert L. Ticknor, North Willamette Experiment Station, Ore.
Russell H. Ireland, Jr., Marin Viette Nurseries, East Norwich, Long Island, N.Y.
Herb Warren, Buchart Gardens, British Columbia
Carl Zannger, American Garden Perry's, La Puente, Calif.

Photographers
Names of photographers are followed by the page numbers on which their work appears.
R=right, C=center, L=left, T=top, B=bottom.

William Aplin: 8B, 9B, 17B
Patricia Bruno/Positive Images: 17T
Michael Dirr: 20TR, 33, 35T, 36, 44T, 45, 46, 47L, 47R, 48B, 49–59, 60R, 61, 62TL, 62BL, 63L, 65R, 67, 68L, 69, 70L, 70BR, 71, 72L, 73, 74R, 75, 76L, 77–82, 83R, 84–87, 88BL, 88R, 89TR, 90, 91R, 92, 93BL, 94–96, 97L, 97BR, 98, 99, 100R, 101TL, 101R, 102, 103TL, 103R, 104, 105, 106L
Margaret Hensel/Positive Images: 28
Saxon Holt: 4, 6T, 7, 9T, 13B, 14, 15T, 15B, 16T, 19T, 19B, 20TL, 20B, 21, 22, 32B, 37, 39, 40, 42, 43, 60L, 62R, 65L, 72R, 76R, 83L, 88TL, 100L, 101BL, 106R
Jerry Howard/Positive Images: front cover, 18, 26, 30B, 31T, 32T, 34, 35B
Sydney Karp/PHOTO/NATS: 44B
Michael Landis: 24T, 27, 70TR
Peter Lindtner: 64L, 66R, 68R
Robert E. Lyons/PHOTO/NATS: 15M, 89L
Michael McKinley: Title Page, 6B, 31B
Ortho Information Services: 13T, 38
Jerry Pavia: 10, 16B, 30T, 74L
Ann Reilly/PHOTO/NATS: 64R
John Smith/PHOTO/NATS: 91L, 103BL
Steven Still: 12, 24B, 25, 48B, 63R, 66L, 89BR, 93R, 97TR
David Stone/PHOTO/NATS: 93TL
Virginia Twinam-Smith/PHOTO/NATS: 8T

Front Cover
This rustic garden path is bordered on the right by mayapple (*Podophyllum peltatum*) and on the left by Japanese spurge (*Pachysandra terminalis*), a widely used ground cover for shady areas.

Title Page
A low-growing violet (*Viola*) border defines and complements this garden path.

Back Cover
Top left: Gazania (*Gazania*) and lantana (*Lantana*) transform a sunny slope into a brilliant backdrop.

Top right: This newly planted woodland garden combines ferns and flowers with periwinkle (*Vinca minor*).

Bottom left: The dense, rounded tufts of Scotch moss (*Sagina subulata* 'Aurea') form a soft, mossy carpet around these stepping-stones.

Bottom right: Sweet woodruff (*Galium odoratum*) is perfect for shady spots, offering tiny white spring flowers and a delicate fragrance.

GROUND COVERS IN THE GARDEN

Ground covers are the practical plants of the landscape—the problem solvers—and are used to integrate and accent the other elements of a garden. To fully appreciate these versatile plants, look beyond their obvious function to their color, form, and texture.

5

LANDSCAPING WITH GROUND COVERS

A well-chosen ground cover can be a useful and attractive addition to any home landscape. This chapter presents some guidelines and ideas for designing with ground covers.

11

All About Ground Covers

BUYING, PLANTING, AND CARE

Plan carefully before buying and planting a ground cover. Select plants suitable for the area, and follow correct planting techniques and maintenance routines. Proper selection and care will result in beautiful plants year after year.

23

PLANT SELECTION GUIDE

This chapter includes lists of ground covers for specific uses. Complete descriptions follow of more than one hundred commonly used ground covers. Use the plant descriptions and photographs to select the ideal plants for your home landscape.

41

Ground Covers in the Garden

Ground covers are the practical plants of the landscape—the problem solvers—and are used to integrate and accent the other elements of a garden. To fully appreciate them, look beyond their obvious function to their color, form, and texture. They are among the most versatile plants in the landscape.

Imagine a tree-shaded bed of rich green Japanese spurge (*Pachysandra terminalis*) or a cool carpet of heart-shaped violets (*Viola*) bordering a walkway. Picture a slope covered in steel blue juniper (*Juniperus horizontalis* 'Blue Chip') or bright green Algerian ivy (*Hedera canariensis*). These are just a few of the uses for the versatile plants known as ground covers—plants that creep, clump, mat, or vine to cover, conceal, protect, and beautify.

Ground covers include all kinds of plants—turf grasses and ornamental grasses as well as low-growing perennials, shrubs, vines, and some herbs. Ground cover plants are valued for their ability to spread rapidly, grow close to the ground, and create a thick covering that binds the soil. They can be deciduous or evergreen, broad-leaved or needle-leaved. They range in size from plants a few inches high to shrubs that reach 3 or more feet at maturity.

Ground covers fill a wide variety of needs in the garden. Because they are more often used as a foundation for other plants, they frequently are underrated in their role as landscape problem solvers and beautifiers. When viewed with an imaginative eye, however, they can do much more than just cover the ground.

A mixed bed of carpet-bugle (Ajuga reptans) *blankets the open area of this unusual garden. In the foreground, shade-loving violets* (Viola) *cover the ground beneath the tree.*

When it comes to less-than-ideal growing conditions or problematic terrain, ground covers can provide the solution. Many ground cover plants are good lawn substitutes and can be used where grasses cannot thrive because of poor soil, dense shade, high wind, or limited moisture. In a heavily wooded yard, for example, where little light penetrates to the ground, ground covers native to the forest floor—including periwinkle (*Vinca*), wintercreeper (*Euonymus*), and goutweed (*Aegopodium podagraria*)—are the answer. For dry conditions, look to plants that require little water: cotoneaster (*Cotoneaster*), juniper (*Juniperus*), and ivy (*Hedera*). All are drought resistant. There is a ground cover to suit just about any type of soil: sandy, clayey, acid, alkaline, moist, or dry. Most of the herb ground covers—such as dwarf rosemary (*Rosmarinus*) or creeping thyme (*Thymus serpyllum*)—do well in poor soil.

Problems posed by specific landscape features also can be remedied through the use of ground covers. Ground covers can blanket and conceal an angled slope or fill in a hard-to-mow space at the base of a tree. A thick ground cover planting can reduce maintenance under trees, because the litter from leaves, flowers, fruit, or bark vanishes into and beneath the cover. This litter eventually breaks down and enriches the soil, to the benefit of both the tree and the ground cover.

Top: Where water supplies are limited, rock cotoneaster (Cotoneaster horizontalis) *and heavenly bamboo* (Nandina domestica) *make attractive and useful ground covers. Bottom: Creeping lilyturf* (Liriope spicata) *is an easy-maintenance alternative to cover the hard-to-mow, shaded area under a tree.*

Ground covers are ideal for preventing erosion on steep slopes, where maintenance is difficult. Ivy (*Hedera*), juniper (*Juniperus*), honeysuckle (*Lonicera*), and periwinkle (*Vinca*) are often used in planting areas such as freeway banks that are difficult and even dangerous to maintain. These plants create appealing carpets while controlling erosion. They cover the land quickly and do not require frequent watering or maintenance. Such plants fulfill these same needs in the home landscape.

The small-leaved ground covers can be used to creep into all sorts of nooks and crannies—between the cracks in garden paths, around stepping-stones, in and over stone walls and fences, in an empty corner, or between the exposed roots of trees. Tall-growing or vining types are useful for covering rocks or hiding unsightly areas. Other ground covers serve as barriers or help to direct foot traffic.

Although ground cover plants are used most frequently as problem solvers in landscapes with difficult growing conditions, they should also be considered for nonproblematic locations because of their beauty and ornamental value. The brilliant flowers of many ground covers are a special bonus, and the herbal ground covers offer fragrant foliage. Some plants provide uniform foliage color throughout the year—juniper, for example—whereas others, such as hosta (*Hosta*), die back, supplying foliage color only from spring to fall.

Ground covers create harmony in a landscape. They provide a continuity of coverage that creates a feeling of tranquility. Mondograss, for instance, serves as a pleasing transition between a lawn area and a flower bed. Besides unifying a landscape, ground covers can emphasize its patterns and forms. They offer variety in height, texture, and color, and make an exciting contribution to any setting. Spring cinquefoil (*Potentilla crantzii*), with its small yellow flowers and dark green foliage, serves as a colorful alternative to a grass lawn. Small-leaved plants, such as baby's tears (*Soleirolia soleirolii*) and lemon thyme (*Thymus* × *citriodorus*), which hug the ground and creep between cracks and crevices, can

Gazania (Gazania) *and lantana* (Lantana) *transform a sunny slope into a brilliant backdrop.*

Top: Sturdy, colorful, and requiring little maintenance, creeping juniper (Juniperus horizontalis *'Bar Harbor') and stonecrop* (Sedum × *'Rosy Glow') create a pleasing combination. Bottom: Mondograss* (Ophiopogon) *is used to frame the lawn area in this garden.*

soften the edges of bricks or stonework and help to blend garden paths into the rest of the landscape.

Ground covers can also be used as attractive accents and to highlight other landscape elements. Used in combination, they create variety in depth and texture. The glossy leaves of ivy (*Hedera*) contrast interestingly with the soft blue-gray matte effect of juniper (*Juniperus*). Scotch moss (*Sagina subulata* 'Aurea') adds pleasing color and a texture contrast to weathered wood.

HOW TO USE THIS BOOK

This book is designed to help you choose the best ground covers for your home landscape. It provides practical information necessary to successfully grow healthy, attractive ground cover plants, and focuses on their special needs. It includes suggestions about the diverse landscaping possibilities that ground covers offer and provides descriptions and photographs of hundreds of ground covers and their cultural requirements.

For a short course in designing with ground covers and using them to their best advantage, read the chapter on landscaping with ground covers, beginning on page 11. This chapter begins with an overview of lawns as ground covers, including their advantages, drawbacks, and possible alternatives. It also contains a discussion of why many ground cover plants require only limited watering once established, and how this can be used to great advantage. Also covered is information on the labor-saving (and time-saving) aspects of nonlawn ground covers, the traditional uses of ground covers in the landscape, and some of the more creative ways that ground covers can be used in a home garden.

The practical information you need to grow healthy ground cover plants is contained in the chapter on buying, planting, and caring for ground covers, beginning on page 23. Here are details on selecting and purchasing plants, tips on preparing the soil, and a description of the essential steps involved in planting. Also included is information on fertilizing, weeding, watering, and mulching, a discussion of ongoing maintenance practices (mowing, pruning), and an overview of plant propagation techniques.

The Gallery of Ground Covers, beginning on page 54, lists 126 of the most widely used ground cover plant species and hundreds of varieties and cultivars. In addition to descriptions and photographs, specific information on each plant's culture and uses is included. This section is preceded by lists of ground covers to suit a variety of purposes and circumstances. Whether the location to be covered is shady, sloped, or in full sun, there are ground cover plants well suited to each condition. If the objective is to restrict access to an area or to replace a lawn, there is a wide variety of ground covers to fulfill those requirements as well. The Plant Selection Lists begin on page 43.

Sweet alyssum (Lobularia maritima) *and periwinkle* (Vinca) *ease the transition between lawn and surrounding shrubs.*

Irish moss (Sagina subulata), *Scotch moss* (S. subulata *'Aurea'*), *and sweet alyssum* (Lobularia maritima) *fill in the nooks and crannies in this terraced garden.*

Landscaping With Ground Covers

A well-chosen ground cover can be a useful and attractive addition to any home landscape. A lawn is the most common ground cover but is not the only alternative. Use ground cover plants to save on maintenance time, to conserve water, and to help camouflage and stabilize uneven terrain. This chapter presents some guidelines and ideas for designing with ground covers.

The ideal landscape could be defined as one in which the viewer isn't aware of any one element, a setting in which a balanced blending of diverse plant materials creates a harmonious, tranquil mood. Ground covers are often used to unify and harmonize a landscape. Their variety of growth habits, foliage, color, and texture, and their range of cultural requirements allow them to fit into any setting. Ground covers blend so well into the outdoor environment that we often take them for granted. But without this versatile group of plants, the landscape would be starkly incomplete.

Every home landscape needs contrasts and accents to keep it from becoming monotonous. Visual focal points brought about by plant color, shape, or texture create interest in the landscape by capturing the viewer's attention. Such focal points can be achieved with individual ground cover plants or by mass plantings. A ground cover planted adjacent to a lawn will break up the expanse of green, adding interesting lines and textures. Splashes of ground cover color—including different shades of green—against stone walls, along paths and steps, or between specimen plants will create the needed contrasts and variety.

Ground covers offer endless variety and interest in the landscape. Here, lavender-cotton (Santolina chamaecyparissus) *provides an intriguing accent to the large rocks that form the focal point of this garden.*

In their role as decorative accents, ground covers may provide practical solutions to small problem areas—for example, bugleweed (*Ajuga*) plants grouped to cover the exposed roots at the base of a tree. But use any accent plant with restraint. Too many varieties with contrasting colors and textures will create a hodgepodge rather than an attractive, integrated landscape.

LAWNS AS GROUND COVERS

Front and back yards, carpeted with grass, are a common sight throughout the suburbs of the United States and southern Canada. Grass is the most widespread and most durable plant material used to cover the ground.

Lawns are pervasive because they offer some definite benefits—both visual and functional. The smooth expanse of a green lawn is restful and pleasant to look at. A lush lawn makes an ideal background for all other garden features, colors, and textures.

Grass holds the soil against erosion and absorbs the rainfall. It stands up under foot traffic better than any other plant. Lawns are fine floors for play areas—soft underfoot and a cushion under falls. Expanses of turf absorb sunlight, and cool and clean the air. Pavement, on the other hand, reflects sunlight and can raise the temperature and air-conditioning cost for the buildings it surrounds.

In many climates, a lawn is a refinement of natural meadows. In other places, it is completely unnatural, but many people still go to great lengths to maintain it. It is part of our modern image of home.

When to Have a Lawn

There are places and uses for which a lawn is appropriate and others for which it is unsuited. A lawn has drawbacks: It requires substantial investments of time and money to install and maintain. A lawn needs mowing every week for at least half the year—in some climates throughout the year. A lawn requires regular

Lawns are still the most widely used ground cover in home landscapes in the United States and southern Canada.

Top: A lawn will withstand foot traffic and hard use in a way that few other ground covers can.
Bottom: Surrounded by native species and other drought-tolerant plants, a lawn can serve as a tranquil island of green.

fertilizing—an expensive commodity, both in terms of product and equipment, and a time-consuming task. Moreover, regular watering is essential to the upkeep of a lawn. This need presents an ongoing problem in regions where water supplies are threatened and there are laws limiting water use.

A lawn has a place in almost every landscape, but care should be given to its size and use. A backyard is usually planted with a grass lawn—to bear the brunt of a family's recreation. Many ground covers will take some traffic also, but not the kind delivered by active children, so they are of limited use in a backyard. Since a front lawn is usually a showcase, however, grown and maintained for visual rather than functional reasons, why not try a ground cover there, to provide the desired carpet of green without the maintenance that is required by a grass lawn? Ground covers offer more than grass visually—a range of foliage and blossom colors and foliage textures.

A lawn can serve as a small design element within the landscape. Connected ribbons, circles, and pockets of lush and velvety lawn are much more interesting and attractive than wide expanses of grass that only a full-time greenskeeper could maintain. The care of a lawn of reasonable extent must be consistent, but it need not be overly time- or energy-consuming. It can be a relief to the homeowner as well as to the environment to limit lawn size and thus the time and cost associated with its care.

Lawn Alternatives

Most people think of a lawn as something everyone has and anyone can grow. Many new houses have a fringe of shrubs, two shade trees, and grass to cover the remainder of the yard.

With foresight and planning, grass can be used to better advantage. Place a sprinkler in the center of the area where turf is most desirable (a part of the backyard or a play area) and turn it on high. Let the area that gets wet be the lawn—and be creative with the edges. Some nonliving alternatives for framing or highlighting a lawn are mulching with bark, wood chips, or other attractive and natural-looking material, or adding outdoor living areas—decks, patios, or paved areas. These make an excellent return in convenience and low maintenance. Another alternative is to use rock mulching for accent and contrast,

especially under trees and along walkways. Put weed mat or mulching cloth under the rock to keep out grass and weeds. Use rocks of various sizes to create different effects—serene or bold, rugged or smooth.

Consider also ground cover plants as a lower-maintenance alternative to a lawn. Ground covers can make nonlawn areas more attractive, interesting, and enjoyable. Best of all, landscaping with ground covers is neither complicated nor time-consuming.

There are fewer than a dozen grasses commonly used for lawns. In many places none of these is practical. In contrast, there are hundreds of ground cover plants, many described in the gallery section of this book (see pages 54 to 106). Among these are plants that tolerate more shade than any of the lawn grasses and also drier or wetter soil conditions. There are plants with fragrant foliage, and those with dense or prickly stems that discourage unwanted entry of both people and small animals. Some ground cover plants offer variety in foliage color; others are covered with lovely blooms for weeks or months at a time. Many ground cover plants have fewer pest and disease problems than lawn grasses. Only a few ground covers need mowing, and those only once or twice a year.

Above: Where foot traffic is light, some species of yarrow (Achillea millefolium *is shown here) make an attractive lawn substitute. This site is further enhanced by the adjoining rockroses* (Cistus) *and lavender* (Lavandula).
Top right: Certain ground covers work well in a variety of locations. Lavender (Lavandula), *rosemary* (Rosmarinus), *and starjasmine* (Trachelospermum jasminoides) *are used to great advantage along these steps.*
Center right: The brilliant carpet of pink Ruschia spinescens *and yellow gazania* (Gazania rigens) *serves to limit erosion on this slope.*
Bottom right: Dwarf coyotebrush (Baccharis pilularis) *is a very effective slope stabilizer for the western states.*

GROUND COVERS AS PROBLEM SOLVERS

A well-chosen ground cover can be used to solve what might at first appear to be a difficult landscape dilemma—a steep slope, for instance. Use ground cover plants on irregular terrain to prevent erosion and runoff. Where water conservation is a priority, choose from among the numerous ground cover plants with minimal water requirements. If gardening time is limited, consider ground cover plants as a lower-maintenance alternative to a lawn and most other landscape elements.

Handling Slopes

Ground covers provide a practical solution for slopes. Carefully selected and properly planted, they can transform a hillside into a gardening asset. For a multitiered effect, a slope can first be terraced to limit erosion, and then planted with your choice of a wide variety of possible ground covers. Or turn a hillside into a living backdrop for color displays of interplanted bulbs, flowering shrubs, and trees by protecting the erosion-prone soil with a ground cover carpet. This will hold the topsoil essential to the other plants in place, thereby strengthening the entire planting.

There are quite a few attractive ground covers that effectively protect a hillside against erosion. (See page 49 for a listing of some of the best slope stabilizers.) Most require minimal maintenance once established. Vining ground covers, such as ivy (*Hedera*), are excellent soil protectors. Cuttings often can be planted directly on the slope. With heavier ground covers, such as juniper (*Juniperus*), it is sometimes necessary to build individual terraces to hold the plants in place until they become firmly established.

Erosion remains a threat until a ground cover has fully developed its root system and foliage to cover the bare soil. In the meantime, cover the slope with netting (jute, available in retail nurseries) to stop the runoff. Install a drip system (see page 35) to water the ground cover most efficiently.

Conserving Water

Lawns require more water than almost any other type of planting. In some areas, certain types of lawn grasses when found in their natural state go almost dormant during the heat

Top: Wild lilac (Ceanothus), *a western native, is among the most drought tolerant of ground cover plants.* Ceanothus gloriosus *'Anchor Bay' is shown here.*
Bottom: The sedums, here, Sedum rubrotinctum, *are often used in southwestern gardens because their water needs are minimal.*

and drought of high summer. Keeping these grasses green requires frequent and heavy waterings—especially in the western and southwestern United States.

Ground covers—like all plants, even drought-resistant ones—need some water some time. And all plants need careful watering until their root systems become well established. But even during this initial period of several weeks to months, ground cover plants will thrive on a fraction of the water needed for a new lawn. Soil that has been enriched with organic matter and has been well mulched before planting (see page 32) will make better use of natural rainfall or of the water applied, further conserving this precious commodity.

Once the ground cover has put down its roots and begun to spread, give it deeper but less frequent waterings to encourage deep rooting. Given this moisture as needed, an expanse of ground cover plants will suffer no periods of summer dormancy as grasses do. Rather, the ground cover will continue to thrive with rich color from spring until freeze, or the year around in frost-free regions. The cut in your residential water bill and the increase in the attractiveness of your family's personal surroundings are repeated dividends.

Top: Careful planning and good soil preparation will ultimately save maintenance time. This heather (Calluna, Erica) *garden requires very little care to look its best.*

Bottom: Once a ground cover spreads sufficiently, it will crowd out weeds. Weeding and the use of weed controls are unnecessary in this bed of Asiatic jasmine (Trachelospermum asiaticum) *and variegated wintercreeper* (Euonymus fortunei 'Gracilis').

Saving Maintenance Time

Home landscapes should offer rest and relaxation to busy people, not more work and more stress. Limiting lawns to a workable size and using ground covers elsewhere is one way to achieve this.

Invest time at the outset, preparing the soil. Thorough soil preparation is as vital to a ground cover planting as it is to any other planting. The plants must be just as carefully planted, and then watered as needed until they settle in and show new growth. After that they will need some additional watering and perhaps some fertilizer on occasion. See pages 23 to 39 for step-by-step guidelines for selecting, planting, and maintaining ground covers.

Weeding can be a problem for the first few seasons until the ground cover spreads enough to crowd out the weeds. Mulch reduces weeding—and watering—to a minimum and makes any weeds that do come up easier to pull.

Ground cover plantings give satisfaction as they spread and grow. Homeowners will have more time to rest and enjoy their yards and gardens, take more pride in the appearance of their property, and experience happy relief from the frustration and demands of excessive lawn chores.

OTHER USES FOR GROUND COVERS

Home gardeners tend to think of plants as belonging in specific categories. Ground covers are obviously cover-the-ground plants, but that is only the beginning. Looking beyond a ground cover's traditional use opens up many creative possibilities. All it takes is the desire to do something different. Ground covers can satisfy nearly all the senses—touch, taste, smell, and sight—so give your imagination free rein in putting these versatile plants to use.

Drape, Trail, and Climb

Some ground covers climb or trail as easily as they spread along the ground. For example, woolly thyme (*Thymus pseudolanuginosus*) can be encouraged to cover an old log, and Virginia creeper (*Parthenocissus quinquefolia*) can add character and color to a brick wall. Wintercreeper (*Euonymus*) can climb to frame a doorway, and creeping-charlie (*Lysimachia nummularia*) can trail to fill in the nooks and crannies in a rock garden.

Look at ground covers with a discriminating eye. Is a particular plant best at eye level, or better to look up at or down upon? Carefully consider the plant's form and growth habit in

Left: This low-maintenance, low-moisture garden combines creeping manzanita (Arctostaphylos uva-ursi), *heather* (Calluna, Erica), *stonecrop* (Sedum), *and roses* (Rosa rugosa).
Top: The dense, rounded tufts of Scotch moss (Sagina subulata 'Aurea') *form a soft, mossy carpet around these stepping-stones.*
Bottom: The many varieties of juniper make this ground cover a sturdy, useful, and attractive addition to any home landscape. The yellow-tipped Juniperus chinensis *'Pfitzerana Aurea' is shown here.*

Top left: Evergreen candytuft (Iberis sempervirens) is blanketed with showy white flower clusters in early spring.
Top right: English ivy (Hedera helix) is equally at home covering stone and brick buildings as it is on the ground.
Bottom: Because Scotch heather (Calluna vulgaris) can withstand full sun, salt air, and windy locations, it is an ideal ground cover for coastal areas.

Many herbs make glorious ground covers. Sweet woodruff (Galium odoratum) *is perfect for shady spots, offering tiny white spring flowers and a delicate fragrance.*

terms of the vertical dimension, since what grows horizontally on the ground might do some interesting things when planted where it will drape or climb.

Ivy (*Hedera*) does equally well trailing down a steep slope or vining along a porch or trellis. Cotoneaster (*Cotoneaster*) adds texture as it spills over a stone wall. Honeysuckle (*Lonicera*), when planted in a hanging basket and left to its own devices, may twine itself into a giant green braid.

Make use of the myriad colors and color combinations of all kinds of ground covers: a yellow-tipped juniper (*Juniperus procumbens* 'Variegata'), a silver-edged thyme (*Thymus vulgaris* 'Argenteus'), or a white-tinged periwinkle (*Vinca minor* 'Argenteo-variegata'). Plant variegated varieties in a window box and let them drape in colorful contrast against the house. Create a spring bouquet of periwinkle and pansies, or mix green ground covers trailing over the front of a planter with bright yellow snapdragons or red zinnias behind them.

Build a lath arch or trellis around a window and let honeysuckle (*Lonicera*) frame the view. Plant dwarf firethorn (*Pyracantha*) in a window box below the arch. Hummingbirds will come for the honeysuckle nectar and other birds for the bright red firethorn berries.

Make a living checkerboard of Irish and Scotch moss (*Sagina subulata*), try designing a garden patchwork quilt combining different covers, or create a tiny Japanese garden. Check the Plant Selection Lists, beginning on page 43, for ground covers suited to a variety of uses.

Herb Covers

Botanically, an herb is a nonwoody plant. In more popular usage, an herb is a plant that is valued for some culinary, cosmetic, or medicinal purpose. The latter definition permits inclusion of many nonherbaceous (woody) plants—lavender (*Lavandula*) and rosemary (*Rosmarinus*), for example.

By either definition, many herbs fit smoothly into the role of ground covers. Herbs offer numerous assets: They display interesting textures and patterns, provide fragrance and color, and are generally easy to grow. Many are sturdy and hardy with regard to temperature. The basic horticultural requirements for most herbs are light, well-drained soil and full sun. As for their limitations, most herbs are for looking at, not walking on—they are usually too delicate or too tall for traffic. Although some herbs can become weedy under favorable garden conditions, shearing (removing the tips of the foliage using hedge shears or power trimmers) keeps them nicely under control.

The "Plant Selection Guide" contains a list of herbs that are star performers as ground covers (see page 53). For details on culture and uses, check the individual listings in the gallery section.

Buying, Planting, and Care

Plan carefully before buying and planting a ground cover. Select plants suitable for the area, and follow correct planting techniques and maintenance routines. Proper selection and care will result in beautiful plants year after year.

Whether the ground cover will replace a problem lawn, cover a barren hillside, frame a flower garden, or drape over a stone wall, an understanding of the basic steps that are the key to growing healthy, vigorous plants is essential. Of primary importance is the initial plant selection.

There are hundreds of possible ground covers: The variety in color, texture, and size is tremendous. A ground cover must be attractive, but even more important, it must be suitable for the particular site to be planted. Match the cultural requirements of the plant with the location to ensure success.

Know the growth habit, mature size, and water requirements of any ground cover before planting. It is possible to experiment with different plants for different locations; ground covers are a highly adaptable group. If the ground cover is to solve a landscaping problem, however, choose carefully for fast and reliable results.

Use the descriptions and photographs in the Gallery of Ground Covers, beginning on page 54, to become familiar with some of the many plants available and how to grow them. Then select a ground cover that best suits your needs.

Select plants and prepare sites carefully before planting. As with the lilyturf (Liriope) *shown here, proper spacing at planting time is also important.*

Top: Check with a nearby nursery for plants best adapted to local conditions. Bottom: Good color and vigorous growth indicate a healthy plant. The tussock bellflowers (Campanula carpatica 'Blue Chips' and C. c. 'White Chips') are thriving at this nursery.

BUYING GROUND COVERS

Sometimes friends or neighbors offer to share starts, cuttings, or divisions of ground covers from their own plantings. Be sure that these are healthy and not too invasive before accepting the offer. Consider first the advantages of buying plants from local nurseries. Ask the nursery staffers questions—they are familiar with the area and the plants. Look at and compare the wide spectrum of available plant choices. Find plants with good color, vigorous growth, and a dense, compact shape rather than long, leggy stems.

Inspect the undersides of the leaves and their junction with the stem to be sure that there is no disease or insect infestation. Ask a salesperson to knock a sample plant out of the pot and show you the root system. There should be plenty of roots, but not so many that they are matted and circle the bottom of the container, almost to the exclusion of soil. (Should you buy plants with matted or circling roots, break or cut apart some of the outside roots before planting.)

Plants can also be acquired through the mail. Purchasing from mail-order catalogs offers two major advantages—a vastly expanded choice of kinds and cultivars, and detailed information about the plant's growth, habits, and ultimate

size and shape—information that can be referred to after planting. Most nurseries carry only the most popular and familiar plants. Catalogs offer dozens or even hundreds more.

Ordering by mail has some drawbacks. Mail-order plants are usually smaller—for easier, less costly shipping. Their arrival date may not coincide with planting plans, and the condition of the plants before and after arrival is always a gamble. Therefore, the reputation of the nursery, the guarantee the nursery offers, and immediate care upon arrival are all very important. Unwrap the plants and check them for water at once. Expose them to light but not to hot sun or wind.

Whether buying plants at a local nursery or by mail, where there is a choice of available sizes and forms, remember that smaller plants are usually less expensive and take less time to recover from moving and transplanting. Larger plants, on the other hand, may save a season or more in reaching maturity or filling in an area.

Choosing a Plant

Ground cover plants are most commonly sold in 1 gallon–sized containers. In general, for most ground covers container-grown plants are better than bare-root plants. Plants are also available balled and burlapped. In some cases, gardeners will start their plants from seed. When buying other than a container-grown plant, the following guidelines apply.

Bare-root plants Bare-root ground covers are available during the dormant season. Many ground cover plants are sold bare root, dwarf periwinkle (*Vinca minor*) and big blue lilyturf (*Liriope muscari*) being among the

Ground cover plants are most often offered for sale in 1-gallon-sized (or less) containers.

Smaller plants recover more quickly from moving and transplanting than do larger ones, although larger plants may fill in faster. Select nursery stock accordingly.

wooden or plastic tray full of ground cover plants. Many are sold this way—spurge (*Pachysandra*) and wintercreeper (*Euonymus*) are good examples. Plants in flats or cells are smaller than those available in individual containers and take less labor, space, and soil mix to assemble. Check the number of plants in the pack. There should be a minimum number of empty spaces. Check for plant vigor and health. Plants from flats with separate sections will transplant with less shock. In an open, unsectioned flat, it may be less disturbing to cut squares of soil and roots for each plant rather than to pull apart the root sections. Such plants will need careful attention during the first week or so until new root growth begins.

PREPARING TO PLANT

The time to plant a ground cover varies across the country. In warm areas, ground covers can be planted almost anytime, if water is available to see young plants through their establishment period. Generally, either a spring or fall planting is best. These are the times of least environmental stress, when the shock of transplanting is most easily endured, temperatures are moderate, and rainfall is most abundant.

In cold-winter areas, spring is usually more successful. Fall plantings are most likely to suffer from the "heaving" caused by the alternate freezing and thawing of the soil. Young plants may literally be pushed out of the ground. With their roots exposed, they quickly die. If you must plant in fall in a northern climate, do so as early as possible to allow the young plants to become established.

Where freezing soil is not a problem, fall planting allows the plants to use winter rains and cool temperatures to become adjusted to their new site. When spring comes, the plants are already established and begin to cover the ground more quickly.

In areas with especially dry summers, avoid planting after late spring unless you are prepared to spend a lot of time watering.

Eliminating Weeds

Before any planting begins, it is essential that all established perennial weeds, such as quackgrass, bermudagrass, and bindweed, be eliminated in areas where ground covers are to be planted. Weeds that are not killed will come back. They will compete with the new plants

most common. Bare-root plants require immediate planting and careful tending for the first several days to two weeks but are often much less expensive to buy and ship.

Balled-and-burlapped plants Shrub-like, woody ground covers, such as spirea (*Spiraea*), cinquefoil (*Potentilla*), and forsythia (*Forsythia*), are often sold as balled-and-burlapped specimens. Balled-and-burlapped plants should have a solid earth ball firmly covered with the burlap. When planting, do not remove the burlap; simply loosen it once the plant is in the hole and then leave it to rot away, taking care that none is exposed above the soil level. If a plastic material is used instead of burlap to wrap the rootball, or a plastic twine to tie it, remove it before planting: Plastic or other synthetic materials will not break down in the soil.

Plants sold by the flat or cell There is usually a price advantage to buying an entire

Space plants uniformly, as in this recently planted bed of Japanese spurge (Pachysandra terminalis).

for nutrients and may even crowd them out. Removal is much more difficult after ground cover plants are in place. Use a systemic weed and grass killer, such as glyphosate, to remove any existing vegetation before planting. Carefully follow all label directions.

Amending the Soil

Ground covers are plants that naturally grow very close together, creating heavy competition for space, nutrients, and water. Starting with good soil helps the plants to overcome these adverse conditions. Soil for ground covers should be prepared as carefully as for a lawn. Extra effort in readying the soil often makes the difference between success and failure.

For proper growth, plants need air in the soil, sufficient moisture, and a supply of mineral nutrients. Clay soils hold nutrients adequately but drain too slowly and leave little room for air. Sandy soils are well aerated but lose moisture and nutrients too quickly.

This newly planted woodland garden combines ferns and flowers with periwinkle (Vinca minor).

The only quick way to improve either sandy or heavy clay soil is through the addition of organic matter. Adding organic matter, such as compost or manure, loosens clay soils, allowing air into the soil and making it easier to work. When added to light, sandy soil, organic matter holds moisture and nutrients in the root zone.

The quantity of organic matter must be large enough to physically alter the structure of the soil. This means that about one third of the final mix should be organic matter. In planting terms, this would be a layer of compost or manure at least 2 inches thick spread over the planting area, worked into the soil to a depth of 6 inches.

It is not practical to spade up an entire yard or a hillside and add the soil amendments. Besides the cost and time involved, the soil becomes more vulnerable to erosion. One solution is to dig a planting hole for each plant (several times wider than the rootball) and fill it with amended soil.

Fertilizing

In addition to amending the soil to ensure adequate drainage, add an all-purpose fertilizer when preparing the planting bed. The first step in using fertilizer correctly is understanding how it is labeled.

All commercial fertilizers are marked with the percentages of nitrogen, phosphorus, and potassium they contain. There are many formulas, but the listings are always in the same order: Nitrogen is first, phosphorus second, and potassium third. A 5-10-10 or 10-10-10 fertilizer worked into the soil before planting will get the plants off to a strong start.

Spread dry fertilizer evenly over the planting hole (this can be done when you add the soil amendments) at the rate called for on the fertilizer label. Work it in with a spade or rototiller. An average amount would be 4 to 5 pounds of a 5-10-10 fertilizer per 100 square feet or 2 pounds of 10-10-10 fertilizer per 100 square feet.

Many fertilizers supply additional elements, such as iron and zinc, that may be lacking in the soil. Test the soil to find out if any trace elements are missing and to determine which fertilizer to use and how much. Soil testing is not always necessary, however. A complete, all-purpose fertilizer will usually satisfy the needs of most plants.

PLANTING

There is no hard and fast rule for estimating the number of ground cover plants needed for a particular location. The spacing guide on this page offers some guidelines. The number of plants also depends on the desired result and the funds available. Naturally, the closer you space the plants, the faster they will cover the ground.

Usually, such plants as English ivy (*Hedera helix*), Japanese spurge (*Pachysandra terminalis*), and periwinkle (*Vinca*) are planted on 1-foot centers (see illustration); cranberry cotoneaster (*Cotoneaster apiculatus*), juniper (*Juniperus*), and wintercreeper (*Euonymus*) on 3-foot centers. Trailing roses (*Rosa*), Virginia creeper (*Parthenocissus quinquefolia*), and other large-scale ground covers are often spaced no closer than 5 feet apart.

Some woody plants, such as junipers, will eventually mound up if they have been planted too close together. If you must space the plants close together to achieve quicker coverage, be prepared to move some at a later time.

In arranging the plants, some gardeners opt for staggered rows, others for straight (see illustration). On slopes, staggered rows are preferred. They help prevent erosion by not allowing water to run off in a straight line.

When planting on slopes, the soil must be held in place until the plants are established. A mulch alone is sufficient in some cases. When the slope is steep, use jute or a similar netting to hold the mulch in place. Jute is usually available in rolls 4 or 6 feet wide. Unroll the netting from the top of the hill and hold it in place with heavy-wire staples (coat hangers are easily adapted to this use).

CARE AND MAINTENANCE

Ground covers are among the easiest plants to care for. There are, however, some basic maintenance requirements that should not be overlooked. These include weed control, thorough watering, and effective mulching.

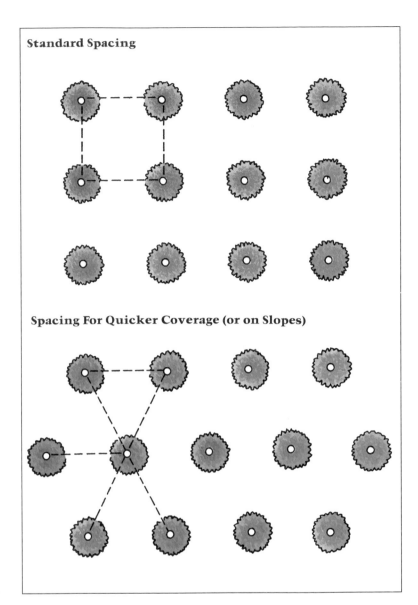

Standard Spacing

Spacing For Quicker Coverage (or on Slopes)

Spacing Guide for Ground Covers

Inches between plants	Square feet 64 plants will cover	Square feet 100 plants will cover
4	7	11
6	16	25
8	28	44
10	45	70
12	64	100
15	100	156
18	144	225
24	256	400

Formulas to determine square feet:
Circles: Area = diameter squared × 0.7854
Triangles: Area = ½ base × height
Rectangles: Area = base × height

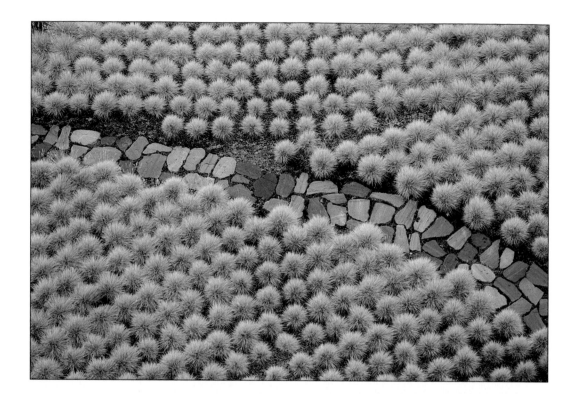

Top: In larger areas, plant blue fescue (Festuca glauca) in regular, geometric patterns rather than at random.
Bottom: As with the junipers (Juniperus) shown here, plant in staggered rows on slopes to prevent excessive runoff.

Top: Mulching is key to successful weed control in planting beds. Bottom: An established ground cover will shade and choke out weeds. Where conditions are right, lily-of-the-valley (Convallaria majalis) *spreads to create a ground cover that needs almost no attention.*

Weed Control

Weeds can quickly overrun any planting and turn an enthusiastic gardener into a frustrated one. The most critical time to weed is just after planting, particularly in spring. Keep a close eye on areas with newly planted ground covers until the plants are dense enough to shade the ground and choke out weeds. And make sure that the planting site is weedfree before setting in any plants (see page 26).

Mulching (see page 32) newly planted beds will help stave off the weed population. Mulches should be applied only after the soil has warmed in spring. A generous quantity will stop many of the most troublesome annual weeds and make it easier to pull ones that do sprout.

Walk through your garden or newly planted area about once a week, taking along a bag and weeding tool. Place all pulled weeds in the bag; if left on the ground they could reroot or spread seeds, causing additional problems.

Certain preemergent herbicides reduce weed populations. For successful weed control using preemergents, read and follow all label directions carefully. In established plantings, use a postemergent herbicide to control grassy weeds without harming the ground cover. Apply any chemical with care, following all the instructions outlined on the label.

Finally, if you desire further information about these or other methods of weed control,

talk to a county agricultural extension agent or local nursery people. They can tell you about the best control methods for weeds specific to your area—and how to apply them.

Mulching

A good mulch is a valuable addition to a new ground cover planting—2 to 3 inches will prevent most weeds from growing. Some of the better mulches are fir bark and tree leaves that have been ground up. There are many others, the availability of which depends on the region. When applying an organic mulch, consider mixing in a balanced fertilizer. Plant roots will often grow into the mulch and the added fertilizer will help sustain them.

Shredded bark   Pine or fir bark makes an excellent mulch that is easy to apply and very attractive. It also adds valuable organic matter to the soil.

Shredded tree leaves   These are an excellent source of humus. They rot rapidly and are high in nutrients. Oak leaves are especially valuable for azaleas, camellias, and rhododendrons.

Rotted manure   Unless at least partially decomposed, manure is high in salts. It is also often sterilized to prevent any weed seeds it might contain from sprouting.

Top: Shredded bark makes an attractive and easily applied mulch, as was done in this garden that combines several varieties of heather (Calluna, Erica) and stonecrop (Sedum). Bottom: Use mulches to conserve moisture— especially important when plants are young and shallow rooted. Shredded bark has been incorporated into this newly planted bed of starjasmine (Trachelospermum jasminoides).

Mushroom compost (spent)   Check for mushroom compost in areas where commercial mushrooms are produced. It is usually inexpensive, and its color blends into the landscape.

Pine needles   In many areas, pine needles will need to be replenished yearly. However, they won't mat down and can take some traffic.

Ground corncobs   Where they are available in large quantities, corncobs, when ground, make an excellent mulch and are very useful for improving the soil structure.

Hay or grass clippings   Although unattractive, hay or grass clippings can be used for mulching purposes. Repeated use builds up a reserve of available nutrients in the soil that will last for years. These may contain grass or weed seeds—be careful.

Straw   Straw is a relatively unattractive mulch and may also contain unwanted seeds. It will, however, furnish some nutrients over time and is especially high in potassium.

Besides preventing weeds from growing, some mulches improve the soil and add nutrients as they decompose. They also conserve moisture, an important consideration where water is in short supply and when young, shallow-rooted plants are just getting started. Finally, they help regulate soil temperature, creating a more favorable root environment.

In areas where winters are especially cold, certain ground covers benefit from a winter mulch. A mulch applied at the time of a new fall planting will prolong the time it takes the soil to freeze, giving the plants a little more time to adapt to harsh conditions. (See page 26 for proper planting times.)

With an established ground cover, apply the mulch after the ground is frozen, to keep it that way. Damage to plants occurs when the soil alternately thaws and freezes. A mulch, such as straw or shredded leaves, loosely applied over the ground cover also insulates plants against drying winter winds. Do not entirely restrict air circulation around the foliage, however.

Watering

Young plants should be given special attention. A steady watering program is important so that root systems develop fully. Watch the plants and make sure that water is getting to the roots. After the plants are growing, adjust the watering program to one of deeper and less frequent watering. This causes the roots to penetrate farther into the soil. Plants then become firmly entrenched in the ground; in a drought situation, this could make the difference in the survival of the ground cover.

Pine needles make a good mulch around these holly (Ilex crenata 'Helleri') plants.

Water plants thoroughly and watch them carefully to make sure that water is getting to the roots.

Water plants thoroughly with a sprinkler. If water is scarce, consider a drip-irrigation system (see page 35). Check the soil to make sure that adequate moisture is being made available to the plants. To do this by hand, simply dig down to the root depth (6 to 12 inches) and withdraw a handful of soil. If it will not form a ball, it is most likely too dry. If it forms a ball that doesn't crumble easily, it is probably too wet. (Sandy soil crumbles even when it is too wet.) Another way to test the soil is with a moisture meter (available at nurseries and some hardware stores). Choose one with a long probe for outdoor use.

Slopes A recently planted slope, particularly one without mulch, is more difficult to water than a planting in a level area. Erosion poses a constant threat. Create small terraces around each plant or terraces across the width of the slope to help control runoff. If erosion occurs, apply the water more slowly. Drip systems are best for watering (see page 35). Mist or fine-spray sprinklers also can be used. Another method is to leave the sprinklers on for 10 minutes (or until the water starts running off) and then off for 20 minutes, giving the water time to soak in. Repeat this until the soil is thoroughly wet.

Drip irrigation   Where water is scarce, use is limited, or rainfall is seldom sufficient for growth of even established plants, drip irrigation offers the most efficient way to use and apply water, especially for the shrublike ground covers. Basic systems are inexpensive and easy to install. Although they can be put in place after planting, it is much easier to put the system and plants in at the same time.

Installing a drip system involves assembling a series of hoses, lines, and emitters or porous tubing that will deliver moisture slowly to plant roots. These can connect with a garden hose or faucet. Drip irrigation waters only the roots so that a minimum amount of water is lost through evaporation. There is less problem with diseases spreading from splashed or wet foliage, and there is no runoff or soil loss because the soil is soaked very slowly. Drip irrigation is ideal for slopes where water applied by other methods often tends to run off before it can sink in.

Top: Once plants fully cover a slope or hillside, erosion is less of a concern. English ivy (Hedera helix 'Spring Grove') is a rapid grower and will fill in quickly.
Bottom: Install a drip irrigation system for efficient water use, as was done on this hillside bed of iceplant (Dorotheanthus bellidiformis).

Basic drip-irrigation kits for small areas are relatively inexpensive. Check the supply sections of garden catalogs or look for companies that specialize in such systems. Their catalogs contain basic information on buying, installing, and maintaining various systems. Drip systems can be automated with timers, and fertilizer injectors can be added to allow feeding and watering in one simple operation.

Drip-irrigation systems can lie on top of the ground or be covered with a few inches of mulch or soil. Place the tubing 12 to 18 inches apart for small plants, 12 inches apart on slopes and in sandy soils. Where temperatures drop below freezing, plastic systems must be taken up before the first frost and the parts drained and stored indoors, as with any hose. Systems with piping made of PVC (polyvinyl chloride, a plastic material) can be thoroughly drained and left in place.

Drip systems are not as practical for closely spaced plants or those that form a solid mass of root or leaf cover, such as Aaron's-beard (*Hypericum*), ivy (*Hedera*), periwinkle (*Vinca*), and some cotoneasters (*Cotoneaster*). For these an underground PVC pipe with fixed sprinkler heads on risers elevated just above the foliage will moisten all the soil beneath.

Mowing

Certain types of ground covers do better if mowed about once a year. This rejuvenates new growth and prevents thatch. (Thatch is a layer of slowly decomposing plant debris that accumulates above the soil and below plant leaves. It stops water and fertilizer from reaching the soil.) Mowing, or any method of cutting back old growth, is very important to the appearance of a ground cover. When a ground cover is beginning to thatch, or the foliage loses

Left: Sprinklers, rather than drip systems, are best for ground covers that form a solid mass of leaf cover, such as the Japanese spurge (Pachysandra terminalis) shown here. Right: Bugleweed (Ajuga) is rejuvenated by light mowing after blooming.

its fresh appearance, it is time to clip off the old growth. Generally, the best time to trim is just prior to the plant's normal growth cycle. This is in spring for most ground covers, just as the weather begins to warm.

Mowing enhances the beauty of carpeting plants such as wintercreeper (*Euonymus*), Japanese spurge (*Pachysandra terminalis*), moss pink (*Phlox subulata*), and bugleweed (*Ajuga*). A mower adjusted to the required height and equipped with a bag for collecting the clipping debris is necessary.

Trimming slopes   Mowing an out-of-the-way area or a steep slope can be difficult or impossible. However, the nylon-line trimmers designed for edging and trimming can be used to some extent for controlling ground covers in difficult terrain. Depending on the toughness of the foliage and the power of the trimmer, this tool can do the job when nothing else can (aside from tedious hand shearing). Keep the trimmer an equal distance from the ground to maintain a level cut.

Pruning   Some ground covers, especially the taller-growing, vining types, can be improved by pruning rather than by mowing or trimming. Using pruning shears on such plants as Oregon grape (*Mahonia aquifolium*) and wintergreen (*Gaultheria*) helps to maintain compactness and the desired dense growth.

PROPAGATING

Occasionally, a bed or slope of ground cover will develop a bare spot, or you may want to extend a planting into a new area. Propagation refers to the many ways of starting new plants, some of which are appropriate for ground covers. For the home gardener, the three most common methods of propagating ground cover plants are by division, cuttings, and layering.

Mossy stonecrop (Sedum acre) and lilyturf (Liriope) are attractive, low-maintenance choices for this pondside location.

The ground covers in this lovely garden can be easily propagated— the sedums (Sedum) *from cuttings and the thyme* (Thymus) *by division or cuttings.*

Division

For the average gardener, division is the simplest method of propagation. To divide clump-forming ground cover plants, pull or cut apart sections of healthy, established plants. Each division (or rooted segment) is itself a plant, or is at least capable of becoming a new one. Divide plants when they are dormant, in autumn or early spring.

Cuttings

Many gardeners propagate new plants from cuttings, always having a few flats ready for repairing planting beds. Softwood cuttings, taken from spring until late summer, are easy to work with and root quickly.

Place the cuttings in a flat or container holding a moistened, sterile medium, such as sand, potting soil, vermiculite, or perlite. A hormone powder (available in many nurseries) applied to the snipped end of the cuttings will help encourage rooting. A greenhouse or cold frame is an ideal location for storing the flats. Otherwise, find a shady, humid, sheltered area, and keep the rooting medium moist (but not soggy) at all times.

Plants vary in how long they take to develop roots. Check the cuttings after a couple of weeks; if the roots are too small or not visible yet, tuck the cuttings back into place, keeping them watered and out of direct sunlight. When the rooted cuttings appear to be growing well, transplant them into individual containers of potting soil. Keep the growing cuttings moist. Gradually increase the amount of sunlight available to them before setting them in their permanent place in the garden.

Layering

To propagate by layering, root the stems or branches while they are still attached to the mother plant. Many ground covers—English ivy (*Hedera helix*), for example—layer naturally. Spring is the best time to start layers. Make a notch in the underside of the stem, about 12 inches from the stem tip. Dig a hole about 4 inches deep and bend the stem into the hole, notched portion toward the bottom. Guide the end of the stem up and out of the hole. Anchor the bent stem in the hole with a wire loop or rock, and fill in the hole with amended garden soil (see page 27). Keep the area moist.

Plant Selection Guide

This chapter includes lists of ground covers for specific uses, from drought-resistant species to those that will tolerate foot traffic. Complete descriptions follow of more than one hundred commonly used ground covers. Use the plant descriptions and photographs to select the ideal plants for your home landscape.

Ground covers of almost any size, shape, habit, and color are available to the home gardener. Many varieties have been developed to meet special needs, and new species, varieties, and cultivars are added every day. Although this guide is extensive, including rock garden plants, hardy perennials, herbs, and plants often placed in the shrub category, it is by no means a complete listing of every ground cover plant. It reflects, instead, a wide variety of hardy, adaptable plants commonly available to home gardeners in the United States and Canada.

Plants are identified in two ways: by common names and by scientific names. Although common names are often easier to pronounce and remember, they are rarely consistent. A plant often has several different common names, varying from region to region, even person to person. A particular common name in one part of the country may refer to an entirely different plant in another.

The *International Code of Nomenclature for Cultivated Plants* is the worldwide authority for horticultural names. The code ensures that every plant has a single scientific name. These names are always in Latin and are divided into two parts. The genus comes first; it is

Decorative ground cover plants such as sunrose (Helianthemum nummularium 'Wisley Pink'), *on the left, ribbongrass* (Phalaris arundinacea var. picta), *in the center back, and lamb's-ears* (Stachys byzantina), *on the right, make a lovely perennial border.*

analogous to a human surname and indicates a general group of plants with many similar botanical characteristics. For example, *Juniperus* is the generic name for a juniper. The specific epithet, which follows the generic name, is a particular category within the genus; for example, *Juniperus chinensis* is a specific juniper, commonly called the Chinese juniper.

A variety is a further subdivision of a species and is distinguished by a plant's ability to pass on its identifying traits through its seed. Varieties occur in the wild. Botanical varieties are indicated in Latin, follow the species name, and are preceded by the abbreviation *var.* For example, *Juniperus chinensis* var. *sargentii* is the Sargent juniper.

A cultivar is similar to a variety, except that it is the product of deliberate horticultural development. Cultivar names follow either the species or variety name and are capitalized and set off by single quotation marks (or the abbreviation *cv.*). They are rarely Latin. *Juniperus chinensis* 'San Jose', the San Jose juniper, is an example. When discussing a generalized group

of plants, often the term *variety* is used more generally to refer both to the botanical varieties and to cultivars.

Plants in this book are listed alphabetically by scientific name; each listing includes the most frequently used common name or names. (Some plants have no common name, however; in other cases, the scientific name doubles as the common name.) Common names also appear in the index, with a cross reference to the proper botanical name.

Each plant entry is followed by the zone number that represents the northern limit of the species' hardiness range. Zones are based on the Climate Zone Map (see page 107) and were developed by the United States Department of Agriculture (USDA). The zone that appears under the genus and common name is that of the hardiest of the species, varieties, or cultivars listed. Where variation within a genus occurs (and this is common), a particular plant's cold tolerance is noted in its description.

Find your zone on the map and use it as a guide when consulting the plant descriptions.

Left: Creeping thyme (Thymus serpyllum) *can take light foot traffic and is very effective between stepping-stones. Coralbells* (Heuchera sanguinea), *on the left, complement the setting.*
Right: This eastern shade garden combines plantain lily (Hosta), *mayapple, colorful azaleas* (Rhododendron), *and ivy* (Hedera).

USDA zones are only a general guide, however: Local conditions of temperature, rainfall, and cultural and environmental factors vary within a region. Check with local nursery personnel to be sure that the plant in question will grow in your area.

Many ground cover plants have numerous cultivars. To simplify the process of ground cover selection, only a fraction of available cultivars is described in this chapter. Moreover, cultivars are best selected to suit regional requirements. Local nursery personnel should be highly qualified to help you choose varieties tailored to the exact requirements of your area.

PLANT SELECTION LISTS

Plants organized by special suitability can be especially helpful if you are searching for a ground cover to fulfill a particular purpose or solve a landscaping problem. Use the lists that follow to direct you to the appropriate description in the Gallery of Ground Covers (beginning on page 54). Note that where an entire genus fulfills the needs of a given situation, only the

Selected Plants for Special Situations

Because ground covers display a wide range of cultural requirements and growth habits, some are naturally better suited than others to specific landscape situations. The lists that follow include ground covers suited to special uses. Check the Gallery of Ground Covers (pages 54 to 106) for complete descriptions of each plant listed.

Hypericum calycinum
(Aaron's-beard)

Coronilla varia
(crown vetch)

genus name is given. In cases where an individual species (rather than the entire genus) is suitable, a specific plant epithet is given.

Ground Covers That Are Sure to Succeed

These ground covers are popular and dependable, will grow in most climates, and are readily available in garden stores and catalogs. Given minimal care, they have proven time and again that they do the job.

Ajuga reptans	Carpet-bugle
Arctostaphylos uva-ursi	Creeping manzanita
Baccharis pilularis 'Twin Peaks'	Dwarf coyotebrush
Cotoneaster	Cotoneaster
Euonymus fortunei 'Colorata'	Purpleleaf wintercreeper
Hedera	Ivy
Hypericum calycinum	Aaron's-beard
Juniperus	Juniper
Liriope spicata	Creeping lilyturf
Ophiopogon japonicus	Mondograss
Pachysandra terminalis	Japanese spurge
Potentilla crantzii	Spring cinquefoil
Rosmarinus officinalis 'Prostratus'	Dwarf rosemary
Sedum	Stonecrop
Trachelospermum	Jasmine
Vinca minor	Dwarf periwinkle

Ground Covers That Spread Quickly

If you prepare the soil well, plant in staggered rows (see page 29), mulch, and water, these plants will fill in quickly. They are ideal for large areas and mass effect. Those marked with an asterisk (*) will take over, given their ideal conditions, and may need to be controlled.

Baccharis pilularis	Coyotebrush
Ceanothus	Wild lilac
Coronilla varia	Crown vetch
Cotoneaster	Cotoneaster
Euonymus fortunei	Wintercreeper
Forsythia	Forsythia, improved cultivars
Hypericum calycinum	Aaron's-beard
Juniperus	Juniper
Lonicera	Honeysuckle
Lysimachia nummularia	Creeping-charlie
Myoporum parvifolium 'Prostratum'	Prostrate myoporum
Pachysandra terminalis	Japanese spurge
Polygonum	Knotweed

Rosa	Rose
Sedum	Stonecrop
Vinca minor	Dwarf periwinkle

Cistus purpureus (rockrose)

Drought-Resistant Ground Covers

Although these ground covers require water and care until they are established, as their roots grow their water needs become less. Eventually, natural rainfall will be adequate for these plants in most areas and years, although they may need infrequent watering in especially dry climates or during long periods of drought.

Aegopodium podagraria	Goutweed
Arctostaphylos uva-ursi	Creeping manzanita
Artemisia	Dusty-miller
Baccharis pilularis 'Twin Peaks'	Dwarf coyotebrush
Cistus	Rockrose
Coronilla varia	Crown vetch
Cytisus	Broom
Festuca glauca	Blue fescue
Genista	Broom
Helianthemum nummularium	Sunrose
Juniperus	Juniper
Lantana	Lantana
Phalaris arundinacea var. *picta*	Ribbongrass
Phyla nodiflora	Lippia

*Helianthemum
nummularium*
(sunrose)

Rosmarinus officinalis 'Prostratus'	Dwarf rosemary
Santolina chamaecyparissus	Lavender-cotton
Sedum	Stonecrop
Verbena peruviana	Peruvian verbena

Ground Covers That Tolerate Full Sun

Plant these right out in the open. They can take the sun full strength. However, in the Sunbelt, many of them do better with some shade, especially in the afternoon.

Achillea tomentosa	Woolly yarrow
Arctostaphylos uva-ursi	Creeping manzanita
Artemisia schmidtiana	Angel's-hair
Baccharis pilularis	Dwarf coyotebrush
Ceanothus	Wild lilac
Cerastium tomentosum	Snow-in-summer
Cotoneaster	Cotoneaster, low growing
Cytisus	Broom
Helianthemum nummularium	Sunrose
Juniperus	Juniper
Lantana	Lantana
Phlox subulata	Moss pink
Phyla nodiflora	Lippia

Pyracantha koidzumii 'Santa Cruz'	Santa Cruz pyracantha
Rosa	Rose
Rosmarinus officinalis 'Prostratus'	Dwarf rosemary
Santolina chamaecyparissus	Lavender-cotton
Sedum	Stonecrop

Ground Covers That Do Well in Sun or Partial Shade

These plants do well whether planted in sun or partial shade. As trees grow and shade spreads, they will adjust without damage.

Aegopodium podagraria	Goutweed
Ajuga	Bugleweed
Bergenia	Bergenia
Campanula	Bellflower
Dichondra micrantha	Dichondra
Fragaria chiloensis	Wild or sand strawberry
Hedera helix	English ivy
Hypericum calycinum	Aaron's-beard
Liriope spicata	Creeping lilyturf
Mahonia repens	Creeping mahonia
Ophiopogon japonicus	Mondograss

Paxistima canbyi	Canby pachistima
Polygonum	Knotweed
Sagina subulata	Irish and Scotch moss
Trachelospermum	Jasmine

Ground Covers That Tolerate Deep Shade

Only a few plants—ground covers or others—thrive in deep shade. Those listed here are particularly well suited to shady areas. Most do not have showy blooms; they are attractive for their foliage.

Adiantum pedatum	Five-finger fern
Asarum	Wild ginger
Aspidistra elatior	Cast-iron plant
Athyrium niponicum	Japanese painted fern
Convallaria majalis	Lily-of-the-valley
Cyrtomium	Holly fern
Dryopteris	Wood fern
Epimedium	Barrenwort
Euonymus fortunei 'Colorata'	Purpleleaf wintercreeper
Galium odoratum	Sweet woodruff
Hedera helix	English ivy
Lonicera japonica	Japanese honeysuckle

Left: Bergenia 'Morgenröte' (bergenia)
Right: Dryopteris goldiana (wood fern)

Top: Euonymus fortunei (purpleleaf wintercreeper)
Bottom: Akebia quinata (five-leaf akebia)

Pachysandra terminalis	Japanese spurge
Sagina subulata	Irish and Scotch moss
Sarcococca hookerana var. *humilis*	Small Himalayan sarcococca
Vinca	Periwinkle
Viola odorata	Sweet violet

Ground Covers for Large Areas

These plants readily spread over large areas and are effective in mass plantings. A few (*Coronilla, Euonymus, Hypericum,* and *Lonicera*) are rampant under optimum conditions and take over if not contained by something like a mowed lawn, driveway, or building.

Aegopodium podagraria	Goutweed
Ajuga reptans	Carpet-bugle
Arctostaphylos uva-ursi	Creeping manzanita
Baccharis pilularis 'Twin Peaks'	Dwarf coyotebrush
Coronilla varia	Crown vetch
Dianthus deltoides	Maiden pink
Dichondra	Dichondra
Duchesnea indica	Mock strawberry
Euonymus fortunei	Wintercreeper

Arctostaphylos uva-ursi (creeping manzanita)

Festuca glauca	Blue fescue
Fragaria chiloensis	Wild or sand strawberry
Hedera	Ivy
Hypericum calycinum	Aaron's-beard
Juniperus	Juniper, low growing
Lantana	Lantana
Liriope spicata	Creeping lilyturf
Lonicera japonica	Japanese honeysuckle
Pachysandra terminalis	Japanese spurge
Phyla nodiflora	Lippia
Polygonum cuspidatum var. *compactum*	
	Japanese knotweed
Potentilla	Cinquefoil
Sedum	Stonecrop
Trachelospermum	Jasmine
Vinca	Periwinkle
Zoysia tenuifolia	Koreangrass

Slope-Stabilizing Ground Covers

These plants hold the soil of banks and slopes in place with their spreading roots and foliage. They absorb water and prevent runoff that could otherwise wash away the soil.

Akebia quinata	Five-leaf akebia
Arctostaphylos uva-ursi	Creeping manzanita
Baccharis pilularis 'Twin Peaks'	Dwarf coyotebrush
Ceanothus griseus var. *horizontalis*	Carmel-creeper

Cistus	Rockrose
Coronilla varia	Crown vetch
Cotoneaster	Cotoneaster, low growing
Hedera	Ivy
Hemerocallis	Daylily
Hypericum calycinum	Aaron's-beard
Juniperus	Juniper, low growing
Lantana montevidensis	Trailing lantana
Lonicera	Honeysuckle
Parthenocissus quinquefolia	Virginia creeper
Phalaris arundinacea var. *picta*	Ribbongrass
Polygonum cuspidatum var. *compactum*	
	Japanese knotweed
Pyracantha koidzumii 'Santa Cruz'	Santa Cruz pyracantha
Rosa	Rose, low growing
Rosmarinus officinalis 'Prostratus'	Dwarf rosemary
Vinca	Periwinkle

Ground Covers That Drape and Trail

The plants listed here tend to grow flat along the ground rather than erect. They cascade over any edge that they encounter or grow gracefully downhill.

Arctostaphylos uva-ursi	Creeping manzanita
Artemisia	Dusty-miller
Campanula	Bellflower

Cerastium tomentosum	Snow-in-summer
Cotoneaster	Cotoneaster, low growing
Euonymus fortunei	Wintercreeper, several varieties
Hedera	Ivy
Juniperus	Juniper, low growing
Rosmarinus officinalis 'Prostratus'	Dwarf rosemary
Trachelospermum jasminoides	Starjasmine
Verbena peruviana	Peruvian verbena
Vinca minor	Dwarf periwinkle

Ground Covers to Fill Nooks and Crannies

Plant these between stepping-stones or patio paving blocks, along walks, or in small areas in which grass would be hard to mow. These plants withstand a footfall now and then and grow slowly enough to edge but not cover.

Alyssum saxatile (*Aurinia saxatilis*)	Madwort
Armeria	Thrift
Campanula	Bellflower

Above: Armeria maritima (common thrift)
Opposite, top: Duchesnea indica (mock strawberry)
Opposite, center: Lysimachia nummularia 'Aurea' (creeping-charlie)
Opposite, right: Galium odoratum (sweet woodruff)

Chamaemelum nobile	Chamomile
Erodium reichardii	Cranesbill
Heuchera sanguinea	Coralbells
Iberis sempervirens	Evergreen candytuft
Lamium maculatum	Spotted deadnettle
Mentha requienii	Corsican mint
Sagina subulata	Irish and Scotch moss
Sedum	Stonecrop
Sempervivum tectorum	Hen and chickens
Soleirolia soleirolii	Baby's tears
Thymus	Thyme

Ground Covers That Tolerate Traffic

These plants do not take as much rough play as grass, but they bear reasonable foot traffic and some mowing to keep them low.

Ajuga	Bugleweed
Chamaemelum nobile	Chamomile
Dichondra micrantha	Dichondra
Duchesnea indica	Mock strawberry
Juniperus horizontalis 'Wiltonii'	Blue-rug juniper
Phyla nodiflora	Lippia
Sagina subulata	Irish and Scotch moss
Veronica repens	Creeping speedwell
Zoysia tenuifolia	Koreangrass

Ground Covers That Tolerate Occasional Traffic

These plants withstand occasional passage without damage but cannot tolerate frequent use. Do not plant them in high-traffic areas.

Achillea tomentosa	Woolly yarrow
Armeria maritima	Common thrift
Cerastium tomentosum	Snow-in-summer
Lysimachia nummularia	Creeping-charlie
Mentha requienii	Corsican mint
Phlox subulata	Moss pink
Potentilla	Cinquefoil
Thymus	Thyme
Vinca minor	Dwarf periwinkle

Ground Covers With Fragrant Foliage

Step on these, sit on them, brush against them between stepping-stones or along the edges of a garden path, and their own special fragrance fills the air.

Achillea	Common yarrow
Chamaemelum nobile	Chamomile
Chrysanthemum parthenium	Feverfew
Galium odoratum	Sweet woodruff

Gaultheria procumbens	Wintergreen
Lantana montevidensis	Trailing lantana
Mentha requienii	Corsican mint
Nepeta	Catnip
Rosmarinus officinalis	Rosemary
Santolina chamaecyparissus	Lavender-cotton
Skimmia	Skimmia
Teucrium chamaedrys	Dwarf germander
Thymus	Thyme
Viola odorata	Sweet violet

Especially Low-Growing Ground Covers

Top: Ajuga reptans (carpet-bugle)
Bottom: Rosa rugosa (rose)

These plants stay almost as short as a lawn but are often more mounded and natural looking. Many offer colorful, seasonal blooms and a

neat, tidy look without frequent mowing. An asterisk (*) indicates those that take some foot traffic.

Ajuga reptans	Carpet-bugle
*Chamaemelum nobile	Chamomile
Cotula squalida	New Zealand brass buttons
*Erodium reichardii	Cranesbill
Euonymus fortunei 'Minima'	Baby winter-creeper
Helianthemum nummularium	Sunrose
Lamium maculatum	Spotted deadnettle
Lysimachia nummularia	Creeping-charlie
*Mazus reptans	Mazus
*Mentha requienii	Corsican mint
*Phyla nodiflora	Lippia
*Potentilla	Cinquefoil
*Sagina subulata	Irish and Scotch moss
Sedum	Stonecrop
Thymus serpyllum	Creeping thyme
Verbena	Verbena
Waldsteinia fragarioides	Barren strawberry

Ground Covers That Create Barriers and Restrict Access

These dense or prickly plants create barriers that deter either people or small animals from walking where they are not wanted.

Berberis thunbergii	Japanese barberry
Cotoneaster	Cotoneaster
Jasminum	Jasmine
Juniper	Juniper
Mahonia	Oregon grape
Microbiota decussata	Siberian cypress
Pyracantha	Firethorn
Rhus aromatica	Fragrant sumac
Ribes alpinum	Alpine currant
Rosa	Rose

Ground Covers for Meadow Plantings

This list includes perennial grasses and wild-flower plants that can be mixed and matched for a meadow effect. Most of these need mowing once or twice a year.

Coronilla varia	Crown vetch
Festuca glauca	Blue fescue
Gaultheria procumbens	Wintergreen
Helianthemum nummularium	Sunrose
Heuchera sanguinea	Coralbells
Lysimachia nummularia	Creeping-charlie
Mitchella repens	Partridgeberry
Perovskia atriplicifolia	Russian sage
Rosmarinus officinalis	Rosemary

Sedum   Stonecrop
Verbena   Verbena

Herbs for Ground Cover

The herbs listed here make useful ground covers. They are also valued for their culinary, cosmetic, or medicinal qualities.

Achillea tomentosa   Woolly yarrow
Alyssum saxatile (*Aurinia saxatilis*)   Madwort
Artemisia caucasica   Caucasian wormwood
Chamaemelum nobile   Chamomile
Galium odoratum   Sweet woodruff
Mentha requienii   Corsican mint
Nepeta mussinii   Persian catnip
Rosmarinus officinalis 'Prostratus'   Dwarf rosemary
Santolina chamaecyparissus   Lavender-cotton
Stachys byzantina   Lamb's-ears
Teucrium chamaedrys   Dwarf germander
Thymus   Thyme

Top: Thymus vulgaris (common thyme)
Bottom: Verbena rigida (vervain)

Abelia × grandiflora 'Prostrata' (prostrate glossy abelia)

Achillea tomentosa 'Aurea' (woolly yarrow)

A GALLERY OF GROUND COVERS

The plant descriptions in this gallery provide a brief introduction to the distinguishing features and best ways to grow, propagate, and use each species. Since it is not possible to predict exactly how a plant will adapt to every particular climate, site, and set of growing conditions, such terms as *fast growing* or *drought tolerant* are relative. A plant that doesn't grow in one location, for example, may thrive in another. Learn about local ground cover plant adaptations and uses not discussed here from local nursery staffers and plant care professionals.

Abelia
Glossy abelia

Hardy in zones 6–9 (to -10° F)

Abelia × grandiflora 'Prostrata' (prostrate glossy abelia) is an evergreen shrub with a spreading, mounding habit and shiny, oval, 1-inch-long leaves that are bronze when new, dark green all summer, and purple-green in fall and winter. Fragrant clusters of small, trumpet-shaped white to pink flowers bloom from early summer until frost. (Few flowers appear in the East and Southeast.) This variety spreads to 5 feet but grows only 1½ to 2 feet tall. 'Edward Goucher' has arching branches and pinkish lavender flowers and grows 4 to 5 feet tall. 'Francis Mason' grows 3 to 6 feet high and wide, its flowers are white with a pink blush, and new leaves are yellow or bordered with yellow.

Culture Glossy abelia tolerates any well-drained soil and responds well to regular moisture and the addition of organic matter. It blooms best in full sun but will take partial shade and moderate salt spray. Plant 1½ to 3 feet apart.

Uses All abelias do well as foundation plantings and in mass shrub plantings. Use 'Prostrata' to mound over a wall or bank, or interplant with other shrubs or among other ground covers.

Achillea
Yarrow

Hardy to zone 2 (-45° F)

Achillea tomentosa (woolly yarrow) is a sturdy, low-maintenance, evergreen herb with narrow, soft, feathery gray-green leaves 1 to 4 inches long. Its growth habit is spreading and rapid. Tight clumps form a dense, matlike cover 8 to 12 inches high. From spring through summer, 2- to 3-inch-wide, flat clusters of tiny golden yellow blossoms appear at the top of 4- to 10-inch-high stems.

Culture Woolly yarrow requires full sun and well-drained soil. It is fairly drought tolerant and needs only moderate watering during the summer. It will not do well in areas with prolonged periods of humidity or regular summer rain. Propagate by seeds or division. Set out rooted transplants 6 to 12 inches apart, preferably in spring. Trim off old flower stalks periodically to help maintain continued flower production. Cut stems back to the ground in fall, at the end of the blooming period.

Uses Woolly yarrow is commonly used in rock gardens and as a border plant. Mowed lightly, it may be used as a lawn substitute where foot traffic is light. It provides erosion control on moderate slopes.

Adiantum
Five-finger fern, maidenhair fern

Hardy to zone 3 (-40° F)

Adiantum pedatum is a hardy maidenhair fern. This beautiful, fine-textured ground cover has 5 frondlets on each of its dark, wiry stems. The delicate, airy fronds grow up to 2 feet tall. The plant spreads by means of creeping rootstalks.

Culture Five-finger fern thrives in shade to partial sun and soil rich in humus. Keep the soil moist and apply a leaf mold mulch (partially decomposed leaves) to prevent

Adiantum pedatum (maidenhair fern)

Aegopodium podagraria 'Variegatum' (variegated goutweed)

Ajuga reptans 'Delightful' (carpet-bugle)

the delicate, fibrous roots from drying out.

Uses This fern does well as an understory ground cover and looks lovely in the shade of trees and shrubs. It may be interplanted with flowers or tucked into the pockets of a stone wall.

Aegopodium

Goutweed, bishop's-weed

Hardy to zone 3 (-35° F)

Aegopodium podagraria (goutweed) is a hardy, fast-growing, deciduous perennial. The leaves are blue-green and usually edged with white. Goutweed forms a low, dense mat 6 to 12 inches high. Clusters of tiny white flowers (resembling Queen-Anne's-lace) on stems 12 to 18 inches high appear in June. The flowers produce seeds that germinate wherever they fall to the ground. Goutweed is very vigorous and apt to become invasive if not controlled. *A. p.* 'Variegatum' (variegated goutweed) grows more slowly and is the most widely planted form.

Culture Goutweed grows in either sun or shade, but growth is slower in the shade, making it more manageable and attractive. It tolerates poor soil and dry conditions. Propagate by seeds or division. Even a small piece of the creeping roots can start a new plant. Mow 2 or 3 times a season to keep the form low and even, and the leaves small and compact.

Uses Goutweed may be mass planted, but management is easiest when it is planted between barriers, such as a sidewalk and a house foundation.

Ajuga

Bugleweed, carpet-bugle, ajuga

Hardy to zone 6 (-10° F)

The ajugas are hardy perennials, long favored by gardeners for their ease of cultivation, fast growth, and showy flower spikes. The ajuga used most commonly as a ground cover is *Ajuga reptans* (carpet-bugle). It is fast growing and spreads by creeping stems. Foliage consists of tight clusters of somewhat oval, wavy leaves 2 to 4 inches long that form a thick,

low mat. For a short time in spring, bluish purple flower spikes rise 4 to 6 inches above the foliage.

'Atropurpurea' has bronze leaves and blue flowers. 'Giant Bronze' is faster growing than the species and has larger, more metallic-looking leaves. 'Giant Green' has bright, crisp green leaves. 'Jungle Green' has larger, more rounded leaves of crisp green and flower spikes 8 to 10 inches high. The leaves of 'Jungle Bronze' are slightly smaller and more rounded; growth is also more rounded. 'Rubra' has dark, purplish leaves. 'Variegata' has leaves edged and mottled with pale yellow. 'Alba' has white flowers and green foliage. 'Bronze Ripple' has purplish to bronze leaves and blue-spired blooms. 'Burgundy Glow', sometimes called 'Burgundy Lace', has blue flowers and a white and pink variegation on green and purple leaves. The leaves have a flatter, less shiny texture than the species, and young foliage has a unique rosy hue. Leaves turn bronze in fall. 'Multicolor' is a bright, variegated form with glossy red,

white, yellow, and purple foliage. It is less vigorous than the species. 'Bronze Beauty' is a very fast-spreading semi-evergreen cultivar with metallic bronze purple leaves and violet blue flowers. It forms dense mats that prevent weed invasion. 'Silver Beauty' has leaves variegated with creamy white and green.

Culture The ajugas grow best in partial sun to light shade. The deeper the shade, the larger and more succulent the leaves. Ajugas need well-drained soil to prevent stem and root rot. Propagate by division; plant in spring or fall, spacing divisions 6 to 12 inches apart. Water moderately, more in full sun. Do not allow plants to dry out. In cold-winter areas, protect plants from winter winds. Plants are rejuvenated by mowing lightly after blooming.

Uses Carpet-bugle is particularly effective when planted in the semishade of other plants or buildings. Along a path it provides a cool, rather formal effect. Flowers are a short-term bonus; the plant's landscape value is based on its handsome foliage.

Akebia quinata (five-leaf akebia)

Alyssum saxatile or *Aurinia saxatilis* (madwort)

Arctostaphylos uva-ursi (creeping manzanita)

Akebia

Akebia

Hardy to zone 4 (-30° F)

Akebia quinata (five-leaf akebia) is a twining, deciduous to evergreen vine. It grows vigorously (up to 15 feet each year), especially in mild climates, and has few insect or disease problems. The deep blue-green leaves are divided into 5 leaflets and are borne on 3- to 5-inch stalks. Akebia is evergreen in mild climates; the foliage remains on the plant late into the season in colder areas. Rosy purple flowers appear in spring, and fleshy purple pods may develop.

Culture This plant grows in sun or shade, does better in well-drained soil, and requires moderate watering. Propagate by seeds, cuttings, or root division. In favorable conditions, akebia can be highly invasive and weedy.

Uses Five-leaf akebia is a very adaptable plant. It is useful on slopes or open areas, where its billowy foliage quickly covers bare ground and its deep roots hold the soil, providing some erosion control. It should be planted away from low-growing shrubs, since its aggressive habit can overtake them.

Alyssum

Madwort, basket-of-gold, golddust

Hardy to zone 4 (-30° F)

Alyssum saxatile, also known as *Aurinia saxatilis* (madwort), is a herbaceous perennial with bright golden yellow flower clusters that appear in spring and grayish green leaves 2 to 5 inches long. Madwort grows to about 6 inches high and is often used in rock gardens.

Culture Madwort thrives in full sun and well-drained soil. This plant is easily raised from seed but has a taproot, so it should be transplanted while still young. Madwort self-sows freely once established in the garden. Stimulate compact growth by cutting back stems after flowering. Plant 10 to 12 inches apart.

Uses Plant madwort in a prominent spot in the garden or along a border to show off its brilliant color. It can also be grown in containers and used in suitable spots throughout the landscape. It is very attractive over rock walls and in rock gardens.

Arctostaphylos

Creeping manzanita, bearberry, kinnikinnick

Hardy to zone 3 (-40° F)

Most species of *Arctostaphylos* are shrubs or small trees. A few species are low growing and make attractive ground covers. One of the best for this purpose is *A. uva-ursi* (creeping manzanita), which grows in northern latitudes around the world. It is a sturdy, evergreen, drought-resistant, slow-growing plant that grows 6 to 10 inches high. Branches, which can spread to 15 feet, are covered with oval, leathery bright green leaves up to 1 inch long that turn red where winters are cold. In spring, small, waxy, bell-shaped white or light pink flowers appear at branch ends. Two handsome cultivars are 'Point Reyes', characterized by darker green leaves set more closely together on shiny red stems, and 'Radiant', notable for the bright red berries that appear in fall and last most of the winter.

A few other *Arctostaphylos* species are useful as ground covers, although they are less commonly available than *A. uva-ursi.* One is *A. edmundsii,* a mild-climate California native that is more heat and drought resistant than *A. uva-ursi. A. edmundsii* 'Carmel Sur' is fast growing and forms a dense, 8- to 10-inch-high ground cover.

Culture *A. uva-ursi* and its cultivars need full sun in mild-summer areas and partial shade in hot-summer areas. In summer, water once every 4 to 6 weeks where soil is loose and fast draining; water less often in heavy soil. Propagate by seeds, cuttings, or division. In spring, set out rooted plants 6 inches or less apart to reduce weed growth. Except for pruning out dead areas, plants should be left untouched. In less favorable conditions, creeping manzanita may exhibit fleshy growth. Watch for gall formation on leaves, which indicates the presence

Ardisia japonica (Japanese ardisia)

Armeria hybrids (thrift)

of fungi or insect parasites; check with a local nursery for how to control.

Uses *Arctostaphylos* is effective as a large-scale planting in informal or native gardens. It is also particularly useful on slopes or trailing over a wall.

Ardisia
Ardisia

Hardy to zone 8 (10° F)

Ardisia japonica (Japanese ardisia) is a mostly evergreen shrub (in some regions it dies back in winter and reappears in spring) with attractive, leathery foliage in clusters toward the tips of upright stems, 6 to 18 inches tall. In fall, tiny white flowers bloom in small clusters among the leaves. Flowers are followed by bright red berries the size of peas that sometimes remain on the plant throughout the winter. The leaves are 4 inches long, oval, bright green, and glossy. There are several variegated cultivars. 'Ito-Fukurin' has silvery gray leaves edged with white.

Culture Ardisia requires shade and regular moisture.

They do best in acid to neutral soil. They spread at a moderate rate via underground stems. Set new plants 18 inches apart.

Uses Use these unusual plants in small, shady places and for winter color and accent.

Arenaria
Moss sandwort

Hardy to zone 2 (-50° F)

Arenaria verna, or *A. caespitosa* (moss sandwort), is a mosslike, evergreen, perennial herb. It is sometimes mistakenly called Irish moss (see *Sagina subulata*, page 97). Moss sandwort has small, narrow dark green leaves that form a dense, slowly spreading, 3-inch mat. Tiny white flowers appear in summer.

Culture Moss sandwort does best in partial shade but tolerates full sun. Plant in well-drained soil and water regularly; plants in full sun require more water than those in partial shade. Provide winter protection in cold, exposed locations. Propagate by dividing plants in spring.

Uses Moss sandwort is best used in clumps bordering a wall or planted between stepping-stones. It tolerates light foot traffic.

Armeria
Thrift, sea pink

Hardy to zone 2 (-50° F)

Armeria maritima (common thrift) is a sturdy, evergreen perennial that grows in dense, grassy clumps. It blooms in spring, into summer in inland areas, and even longer in coastal and cooler areas. The delicate pink or white flowers are borne on long, thin stems. Height can range from 2-inch tufts and 3- to 5-inch flower stalks to 10-inch tufts with flowers rising more than 2 feet. Clumps spread slowly to about 15 inches.

The appearance of thrift varies, depending upon soil conditions, exposure, and variety. Because of the number of varieties and natural hybridization, great variation occurs in mature plants. Common varieties are 'Alba' (with

white flowers), 'Californica' (shorter stems, larger flowers), and 'Purpurea' (purple flowers). There are many others.

Culture Thrift thrives in medium shade or full sun and well-drained soil. It requires only moderate watering during hot summer months. To ensure replication, plants are best propagated by division.

Uses Thrift is used in seaside gardens, rock gardens, and as a border plant. Its general toughness, long blooming period, delicacy of flowers, and interesting leaf texture make it useful in many sites. When kept low it can be used between stepping-stones.

Artemisia
Dusty-miller, wormwood, angel's-hair, artemisia

Hardy to zone 4 (-20° F)

These perennial herbs are sturdier than they look. They have lacy, finely cut silver gray foliage and produce tiny, inconspicuous yellow flower heads for a short time at summer's end.

Artemisia 'Silver Brocade' (dusty-miller)

Asarum shuttleworthii (southern wild ginger)

Caucasian wormwood (*Artemisia caucasica*) is sold at some nurseries as 'Silver Spreader'. It forms a dense mat 3 to 6 inches high that spreads 2 feet or more. The foliage of *A. frigida* (fringed wormwood) is whiter and is carried on the upper part of 12- to 18-inch stems that are woody at the base. *A. schmidtiana* (angel's-hair) forms dense, tufted mounds; two cultivars of *A. schmidtiana* differing only in height are 'Silver Mound', about 1 foot tall, and 'Nana', a few inches tall.

Artemisia 'Powis Castle', a more recent introduction, grows 20 to 24 inches tall and up to 3 feet wide. It has gracefully mounding, filigreed silver foliage and no flowers. In full sun, the plant is vigorous and long-lived. This hybrid does best in zones 5 to 8. *A. ludoviciana* 'Silver King' (southernwood) has fragrant, frothy silver foliage. It grows 3 to 4 feet or more in height, spreads 3 feet, and does best in full sun in cooler areas, light shade in the South. 'Silver Brocade' has a very lacy leaf and effect.

Culture   Artemisias thrive in full sun but tolerate partial shade. They need well-drained soil, are drought tolerant, and require only moderate watering. Tall varieties should be cut back or they become rangy. Artemisias do not do well where summers are humid. Propagation by seeds is slow; division is a better method. Plant artemisias in spring, placing low varieties 6 inches apart and taller varieties 12 inches apart.

Uses   Artemisias are used to soften and mesh colors in the landscape. They are especially effective as border plants, where their soft, pale color and interesting leaf pattern provide a contrast to more brightly colored plants or turf areas. They tolerate light foot traffic.

Asarum
Wild ginger

Hardy to zone 3 (-35° F)

The wild gingers are incomparable ground covers for the heavily shaded, woodland soils to which they are native. Although they are not related to culinary ginger, their creeping rootstalks and pungent leaves have a gingerlike fragrance. The 2- to 7-inch-long, heart-shaped leaves are borne on 7- to 10-inch-long stalks. Reddish brown flowers bloom in early spring, below the foliage, and are usually not noticed.

Asarum caudatum (British Columbia wild ginger) is an evergreen species, native to the coastal mountains of the western United States and British Columbia. *A. europaeum* (European wild ginger) looks almost identical to *A. caudatum* except for its shinier, glossier leaves. Both are hardy to -25° F. Other evergreens are *A. arifolium* and *A. virginicum*. They are native to the southeastern United States and are hardy to -15° F. *A. shuttleworthii* (southern wild ginger) has glossy, leathery foliage mottled with silver. It spreads by underground runners. The cultivar 'Callaway' is a vigorous grower with smaller, silver-patterned leaves.

Deciduous types are native to much of the eastern United States but are not cultivated as frequently as evergreen ones because of the lack of winter effect. *A. canadense* (Canadian wild ginger) is one of the most hardy of the deciduous species and can be used as a ginger substitute by collecting and drying the creeping roots. This species tolerates temperatures to -35° F.

Culture   The gingers are native to woodlands where shade is heavy and the soil is high in humus and moisture. Gingers do best in soils that are either naturally high in humus or generously amended. Locations protected from drying winds are best. Propagate by dividing the creeping rootstalks.

Uses   In a naturalistic woodland garden, gingers form an exceptionally attractive, dense mat. Combine them with evergreen shrubs or wildflowers.

Aspidistra elatior (cast-iron plant)

Astilbe chinensis 'Pumila' (false-spirea)

Athyrium niponicum 'Pictum' (Japanese painted fern)

Aspidistra
Cast-iron plant

Hardy in zones 8, 9 (to 10° F)

Aspidistra elatior (cast-iron plant) has large, blade-shaped leaves that form spiky mounds. Leaves reach 18 to 24 inches long and 3 to 5 inches wide and have long, stout petioles (stems that support the leaf blades). The leaves are dark and somewhat glossy with prominent parallel veins and smooth margins. Flowers are small and inconspicuous, appearing at the base of the plants or underground. This evergreen perennial grows in mild areas of the Gulf and western states. 'Variegata' has attractive dark green and milky white stripes on the foliage.

Culture Cast-iron plant tolerates poor, sandy, or heavy soils but does best in enriched, porous soil. It is very shade tolerant and does well in light to heavy shade. It produces more leaves with moderate fertilization and adequate watering but survives drought and neglect. The leaves may yellow or bleach in full sun—remove any faded ones. To speed spreading, divide the rootstock and plant the divisions.

Uses Cast-iron plant is a fine ground cover or an edging plant in shady areas where little else will grow. (It will take more shade than most other landscaping plants.)

Astilbe
False spirea, meadowsweet, astilbe

Hardy to zone 4 (-30° F)

Astilbes are long-lived perennials that add a dramatic touch as a small-scale ground cover. The delicate flowers that appear in spring are the main attraction. A few of the hundreds of cultivars and colors available include × *arendsii* 'Brautschleier', with pure white flowers; 'Cattleya', pink; 'Diamant', white; 'Deutschland', creamy white; 'Fanal', deep garnet red; 'Peach Blossom', pale peach pink; and 'Rheinland', carmine pink. 'Red Sentinel' has bronzy leaves and bright red flowers; 'Federsee' has vivid red flowers suffused with salmon and is especially adaptable to dry areas.

Astilbe chinensis var. *pumila*, one of the best ground covers, has a spreading habit and grows only 4 inches tall. It is flowers are lilac pink. This cultivar also tolerates drier conditions than most astilbes. *Astilbe chinensis* × *hybrida* 'Snowdrift' has 2-foot feathery plumes of pure white flowers.

Culture Astilbes thrive in shade or partial shade; they need some protection from direct sun. These plants grow best in a cool, well-drained soil that is rich in humus. Keep them moist but do not overwater. For best flower display, divide astilbes every 3 or 4 years and fertilize them each spring. Cut them back after flowering. Roots are shallow, so deep-working the soil is not necessary. A mulch is very helpful. Good soil drainage is especially important, because astilbes are very sensitive to water-logged conditions in winter. (Plant in mounds or raised beds to improve drainage.) In some areas, Japanese beetles are a pest. Check with qualified nursery personnel for the best means of control.

Uses Astilbes are attractive near pools and streams and in woodland settings. They combine well with hostas and bergenias.

Athyrium
Fern, athyrium

Hardy to zone 6 (-10° F)

Athyriums are delicate, deciduous, 2- to 4-foot-high ferns. They are very easy to grow. The most common species is *A. filix-femina* (lady fern). It tolerates more sun and less moisture than most ferns and spreads thickly, outcompeting most weeds. It is shaped like a vase and has yellow-green fronds. There are many varieties of this species.

A. niponicum (Japanese painted fern) is also used as a ground cover. The cultivar 'Pictum' is low growing (to 1½ feet) and has slightly drooping fronds, notable for their coloring. The ruby red stems and main veins contrast strikingly with the soft gray-green fronds.

Culture These ferns do best in mild-winter areas but can grow everywhere. Ideal conditions include partial sun to

Baccharis pilularis (dwarf coyotebrush)

Berberis thunbergii 'Kobold' (Japanese barberry)

shade, good garden soil, and lots of moisture. Protect plants from wind or the fronds will become ragged looking. Fronds turn brown and unsightly after repeated frosts.

Uses The lady fern is an excellent ground cover in woodland gardens or along streams. The unusual coloring of the Japanese painted fern makes it an interesting accent plant—use it where it can be appreciated at close range.

Baccharis
Coyotebrush

Hardy to zone 8 (10° F)

Baccharis pilularis (dwarf coyotebrush) is an evergreen shrub that makes an excellent ground cover. It is available primarily in the western United States, where it is native. Leaves are small, lightly toothed, dark green, and closely set on woody branches. The shrub grows at a moderate rate to about 2 feet (sometimes higher with age) and spreads 3 to 8 feet. Inconspicuous flowers appear at the leaf ends in summer. The commonly used cultivar 'Twin

Peaks' is similar to the species but has a lower, more compact growth habit. 'Pigeon Point', a less well known cultivar, is greener, grows faster, and is higher and more mounding. It spreads to at least 10 feet.

Culture *Baccharis* are remarkably adaptable plants, growing equally well in sun or shade and in almost any type of soil. They are known for their drought tolerance, but they also tolerate wet conditions. Propagate by cuttings, spacing the rooted plants 1½ to 3 feet apart in fall; cover the area with a mulch to inhibit weeds. Dead wood and arching branches should be pruned out each spring.

Uses These tough plants grow inland or along the shore and provide superior erosion control. Use them also to cover stream banks or to drape over garden walls. For high-desert gardens, *B. pilularis* is one of the most reliable ground cover plants.

Berberis
Barberry

Hardy to zone 5 (-20° F)

Berberis thunbergii (Japanese barberry) is a deciduous, 4- to 8-foot-high shrub with bright red berries, spiny, arching branches, and brilliant yellow to scarlet autumn foliage. Many of its cultivars have a low or compact growth habit and are therefore excellent ground covers.

'Crimson Pygmy' (often sold as 'Atropurpurea Nana') forms a compact mound about 2 to 3 feet high and 2 to 4 feet across. The foliage consists of red-purple leaves, ½ to 1 inch long, set densely along the branches. The leaves retain their color through spring and summer. Flowers are purple tinged with gold. 'Aurea' has gold flowers and bright yellow foliage and grows in a mound 3 to 4 feet high and 3 feet wide. 'Kobold' is among the lowest-growing cultivars, reaching 1 to 2 feet high at maturity. It has dark green foliage and yellow flowers. 'Rose Glow' makes a rounded mound 5 to 7 feet tall and equally wide. The leaves are rose pink

mottled with maroon red splotches. Flowers are gold.

Evergreen species of barberry are also available. These include *B.* × *chenaultii*, *B. verruculosa*, *B. julianae* 'Nana', and *B. candidula*.

Culture Japanese barberry grows well in sun or partial shade. Red-leaved forms need full sun for the best color to develop. These plants do well in all kinds of soil and need only moderate watering—they are very drought tolerant. Propagate by layering or softwood cuttings.

Uses The low-growing or compact cultivars of *B. thunbergii* are excellent ground covers for gentle slopes, along paths, and in dry, rocky areas. The spiny branches discourage traffic.

Bergenia
Bergenia

Hardy to zone 2 (-50° F)

These common perennials have large leathery leaves and handsome pink, white, or rose flower spikes that appear in spring. *Bergenia cordifolia* (heartleaf bergenia) grows to

Bergenia 'Morgenröte' (bergenia)

Calluna vulgaris (Scotch heather)

20 inches high. The leaves are fleshy, grow to 10 inches long, have wavy edges, and are heart shaped at the base. The flower spikes are 15 inches long. *B. cordifolia* 'Profusion' bears pinkish white flowers in large clusters. 'Perfect' has rosy red flowers above lustrous leaves that persist in winter. 'Purpurea' has large round leaves with a purple flush that turns to maroon in the cold months. 'Redstart' has glossy bronze-colored evergreen foliage and deep carmine to rose flowers.

B. crassifolia (Siberian tea) is similar to *B. cordifolia,* but the leaves are shorter by 2 to 3 inches, are finely toothed, and do not have a heart-shaped base. Flower spikes are taller by 3 to 4 inches and emerge in winter in mild-climate areas. 'Silberlicht' is a semievergreen cultivar. It bears tight clusters of white flowers with red centers on 1-foot-high stems in spring, slightly later than the genus. The hybrid 'Bressingham Ruby' has a rich maroon color

in winter and is glossy green with crimson undersides in summer. Flowers are rosy red. It tolerates more heat than other varieties and does well in zones 3 to 8. 'Bressingham White' has white flowers; 'Rotblum' has dark red flowers.

Culture   Plant bergenias in some shade, protected from the wind. In cool, coastal areas plant in full sun. (These plants do not tolerate high humidity and extreme heat, especially high nighttime temperatures.) Bergenias grow best in a well-drained soil that is kept moist. Cut the plants back when the thick, woody rhizome (a modified stem that grows along the soil surface) becomes leggy. If clumps become crowded, divide them. Water and fertilize regularly. Bait for snails and slugs if necessary.

Uses   Bergenias are commonly used for shady borders, in clumps among smaller-leaved ground covers, around irregular surfaces such as rocks, and by pools and streams. They combine well with ferns, hostas, and tall rhododendrons.

Calluna
Scotch heather

Hardy to zone 4 (-20° F)

Calluna is one of three genera (*Erica* and *Daboecia* are the others) that constitute the heaths and heathers. The many varieties of *C. vulgaris* (Scotch heather) are somewhat hardier than the heaths and have smaller, overlapping, evergreen leaves that are suggestive of junipers. They also grow taller—some varieties reach 2 feet. Different leaf colors are available, ranging from yellow gold, red, silver, and bronze to the familiar rich green. The tiny, bell-shaped flowers are about ¼ inch long and come in many shades of red and white—rose is typical.

Culture   The requirements of Scotch heather are the same as those of heaths (see *Erica,* page 71). Heathers may be somewhat slower growing than heaths, however, so plants should be spaced closer to one another—about 1 foot apart. Use a mulch to control weeds until the cover is established. These plants do not do well in the southern United

States and wherever summers tend to be moist and humid and temperatures remain high during the night.

Uses   The low-growing heathers are useful as borders and edging plants as well as ground covers. Their deep roots help prevent soil erosion on steep slopes. Heathers can withstand salt air and exposed, windy locations and are therefore well suited to coastal locations. Like heaths, they require very little maintenance once established.

Campanula
Bellflower

Hardy to zone 3 (-40° F)

The nearly 300 species of *Campanula* are characterized by bell- or star-shaped flowers in various shades of blue. *C. garganica* (Adriatic bellflower) is the lowest growing. It forms a loose, 3- to 6-inch-high mat of heart-shaped green leaves, 1½ inches wide, that grow at the end of spreading stems. The plant blooms from late summer into fall, producing many star-shaped violet blue flowers.

Campanula carpatica (tussock bellflower)

Delosperma cooperi (iceplant)

Ceanothus prostratus (squawcarpet)

C. poscharskyana (Serbian bellflower) is similar but taller, reaching up to 1 foot in height. Its flowers, also star shaped, display a more lavender hue. It has a trailing growth habit, spreading rapidly by creeping runners. *C. carpatica* or *C. turbinata* (tussock bellflower) grows in compact, leafy tufts, usually to about 8 inches tall. Flowers are blue or white, bell or cup shaped.

Culture   In cold climates and coastal areas, these plants grow best in full sun; in warmer climates, they need light shade. Bellflowers are sturdy plants that grow well in almost any soil with good drainage. In dry-summer areas, they require watering 2 or 3 times a month. Propagate by seeds or by dividing plants in spring; space new plants about 10 inches apart. Bellflowers can be invasive and should be contained or separated from other plants by a header or divider. These plants do not grow in the southern United States.

Uses   These low-growing bellflowers are best for small-scale plantings; both need to

be seen up close to be appreciated. Adriatic bellflower is attractive in the filtered shade of a large tree, such as a sycamore, where it will grow among the exposed roots. It is also effective spilling over a stone wall. Serbian bellflower is lovely as an accent plant in any shaded garden area.

Carpobrotus, Delosperma, Lampranthus
Iceplant

Hardy to zone 5 (-20° F)

There are many different iceplants—ones that spread, trail, or are bushy. All are sturdy, almost maintenance free, colorful, and drought resistant. *Carpobrotus edulis* (sea or hottentot fig) has daisylike flowers that vary from pale yellow to deep pink. The plants have a trailing growth habit, succulent leaves, and edible figlike fruits in fall. *Delosperma* 'Alba' (white trailing iceplant) is fast growing and widely available. An almost continuous bloom of small white flowers provides color contrast to the green leaves. *D. nubigenum* and *D.*

cooperi are common eastern iceplants. They are quite cold tolerant and do well from zones 5 to 10. *D. nubigenum* forms a thick carpet of cylindrical bright green leaves that turn red in fall and stay red until spring. At that time yellow flowers, 1 to 2 inches in diameter, cover the plant for several weeks.

Lampranthus species are the most common of all the iceplants. They range from 10 to 15 inches in height and produce masses of showy, brilliantly colored, daisylike flowers. *L. aurantiacus* is a bushy plant with predominantly orange flowers. 'Glaucus' has yellow flowers; 'Sunman' has yellow-orange ones. All bloom from late February into May with a scattering of flowers through the summer. *L. productus* spreads from 18 to 24 inches and blooms from January through April. Flowers are purple and 1 inch wide. *L. spectabilis* (trailing iceplant) produces masses of flowers that cover the foliage in spring. Trailing iceplants are available in pink, rose pink, red, and purple. Flowers

are about 2 inches across and plants are 6 to 12 inches high.

Culture   Iceplants do best in porous soil and full sun. They are propagated by cuttings or divisions spaced 12 to 18 inches apart. In arid climates, water 2 or 3 times during the dry season to keep plants healthy. Watch for scale, a serious problem in iceplant. Control with appropriate sprays, used carefully.

Uses   Iceplants are effective in mass plantings covering level ground or slopes. They are also excellent for erosion control on steep slopes.

Ceanothus
Wild lilac

Hardy to zone 7 (0° F)

Several low-growing species of *Ceanothus* make beautiful ground covers. These evergreen shrubs are native to the western United States and are available mainly in that area. These plants are not related to true lilacs but get their common name from their lilaclike blossoms. *C. gloriosus* (Point Reyes ceanothus) forms a dense, evergreen mat, 1 to 1½

Cerastium tomentosum (snow-in-summer)

Ceratostigma plumbaginoides (dwarf plumbago)

feet high, spreading slowly to about 5 feet. The leaves are leathery, dark green, 1½ inches long, and mostly round. The plant blooms in late spring, producing clusters of violet blue flowers.

C. griseus var. *horizontalis* (Carmel-creeper) forms a dense cover 1½ to 2½ feet high and spreads 5 to 15 feet. It produces violet blue flower clusters 2 to 3 inches long. 'Compacta' grows only 1 foot high. *C. prostratus* (squaw-carpet) is the lowest-growing wild lilac, forming a dense mat about 3 inches high that spreads to 10 feet wide. It has the typical leathery, small, roughly edged dark green leaves and small, rounded clusters of blue flowers.

Culture Wild lilacs need a sunny location and light, well-drained soil. Good drainage is important; these plants do not tolerate wet conditions. In a home garden they can develop root rot from receiving more water than they would in the wild. Wild lilacs are difficult to propagate by seeds and cuttings. It is best to buy the plants from nurseries, where it

is possible to check the numerous varieties available. Wild lilacs cannot be grown in the southern United States.

Uses These plants are excellent for western seaside gardens, where they are almost maintenance free. With attention, they can often be grown successfully inland. They make fine accent plants in informal settings.

Cerastium
Snow-in-summer

Hardy to zone 3 (-40° F)

Cerastium tomentosum (snow-in-summer) is a popular evergreen ground cover because of its striking light gray foliage, its hardiness, and its adaptability to almost any growing condition. It forms a dense mat 4 to 6 inches high. Masses of slender stems spread along the ground and then turn upward; narrow, woolly leaves ¾ inch long cover the upper sections. The foliage is covered with white flowers, ½ inch in diameter, from spring into summer. This

species spreads about 2 feet each year: A single plant can cover as much as 9 square feet at maturity.

Culture For optimum appearance, plant in full sun and in soil that is well drained. Mow plants lightly at the end of the blooming period to remove dead flower heads. Snow-in-summer is drought resistant but looks better with regular waterings in hot, dry-summer areas. Propagation is easy by seeds, division, or cuttings. Set plants 1 to 2 feet apart in spring.

Uses Use snow-in-summer where its unusual color can contrast well with its surroundings. It is effective on slopes or level ground, or between stepping-stones.

Ceratostigma
Plumbago

Hardy to zone 5 (-20° F)

Ceratostigma plumbaginoides (dwarf plumbago) is an easy-to-grow, wiry-stemmed perennial. It is valued for its long-lasting, ½-inch-wide blue

flowers, which appear in late summer and last into fall. It grows in tufts up to 12 inches tall and spreads rapidly by underground stems. The leaves are dark green, about 3 inches long, and develop a reddish tint in fall. In the mildest climates, some leaves remain throughout the winter, but most die back; new growth appears by late spring.

Culture Dwarf plumbago takes full sun or light shade and tolerates many soil types as long as drainage is good. Supply moderate amounts of water, more if the plants are growing in full sun. Cut plants back in fall, after the flowers have died. Propagate by division in spring, spacing the new plants 1 to 2 feet apart.

Uses Dwarf plumbago is an adaptable plant with many uses. It can cover fairly large areas and is attractive tucked into corners or under shrubs. It combines well with ajuga (page 55) or sempervivums (page 99).

Chamaemelum nobile (chamomile)

Chrysanthemum parthenium (feverfew)

Chamaemelum
Chamomile

Hardy to zone 7 (0° F)

Chamaemelum nobile (formerly known as *Anthemis nobilis*) is an evergreen, perennial herb long popular in Europe as a lawn substitute. During summer, small greenish or yellowish flower heads with white petals appear at the top of slender stalks. Dried, these are often used in tea. Chamomile has lacy, dramatic, lustrous, grass green leaves that form a low, soft mat. The plant spreads at a moderate rate.

Culture Chamomile grows best in light, sandy soil in full sun but tolerates some shade. Its deep roots make the plant drought resistant—it requires only moderate watering in summer. (It does not do well in the southern United States where summers are moist and humid.) Chamomile is easily propagated by division in spring or fall; set new plants 6 to 12 inches apart.

Uses Left to grow to its natural height of 3 to 12 inches, chamomile is an adap-tive plant in small areas of the garden. Sheared, it is attractive between stepping-stones. When kept mowed, it can serve as a lawn substitute or a living, growing path, made more attractive by the pleasant fragrance it gives off when walked upon. For tea, steep dried flower heads in hot (not boiling) water for 10 to 15 minutes. The herb only lightly colors the water—judge strength by smelling.

Chrysanthemum
Chrysanthemum

Hardy to zone 5 (-20° F)

Most chrysanthemums are best suited to the flower garden, but two may be used effectively as ground covers. *Chrysanthemum parthenium* (lately reclassified as *Tanacetum parthenium* and commonly called feverfew) has finely cut medium green, 4-inch-long leaves that give off a spicy fragrance at the slightest touch. The plant is upright in habit and can grow 2 to 3 feet tall as a biennial or perennial. The small, daisylike flowers have flat yellow centers and short rays; they bloom in tight, flat clusters. This rugged plant can grow in a crack in a driveway and come back even after it has been ripped out. Cultivars include 'Golden Ball', with yellow flowers; 'Silver Ball', with white double flowers; and 'Golden Feather', which has chartreuse foliage and grows 8 to 10 inches high.

C. pacificum is a fast-growing plant, forming a solid, weed-inhibiting, foot-high mat that spreads 3 feet wide in three years' time. Leaves are delicately edged in white; clusters of yellow flowers appear in October.

Culture Divide clumps or start seeds in early spring, or take cuttings from October through May. Once grown, these chrysanthemums self-sow freely or can be increased by division or from cuttings that root easily. Sow seed indoors 2 weeks before the last expected frost. Transplant to the garden in June. In mild climates, sow seeds outdoors in early fall and thin to 9 to 12 inches apart in late spring.

These chrysanthemums thrive in dry places; they tolerate full sun to light shade but do best in partial shade. Shear occasionally to keep plants low and compact.

Uses Feverfew seems to repel harmful insects, perhaps because it contains pyrethrum, a natural insecticide. It also deters bees, so keep it at a distance from plants that need bees for pollination (such as squash and cucumber) or from plants grown especially to attract bees. Use feverfew plants for fillers or for contrast among other bedding plants. A tea can be made from feverfew flowers and used medicinally to reduce fever, hence its common name.

Cistus
Rockrose

Hardy to zone 8 (15° F)

The rockroses are fast-growing, evergreen, mostly upright shrubs distinguished by lovely, roselike flowers. Two species are low growing and can be planted as ground covers. *Cistus salviifolius*, often erroneously called *C. villosus*

Cistus salviifolius (sageleaf rockrose)

Convallaria majalis (lily-of-the-valley)

'Prostratus' (sageleaf rock-rose) has delicate white flowers with yellow spots at the base of the petals. Flowers appear in profusion from late spring into midsummer. Leaves are gray-green, rather small, oval, and sparsely hairy. Mature shrubs reach 2 feet in height and spread to about 6 feet.

C. crispus (wrinkleleaf rockrose) is a distinctly prostrate, rigidly branched species, growing to a maximum height of 18 inches. It has deep green foliage with wavy leaves that are slightly aromatic when crushed. Flowers are a striking red-pink with a bright yellow center. They are the same size as those of *C. salviifolius* (1 to 1½ inches wide) and have the same late-spring to midsummer blooming period.

Culture Rockroses are sun-loving plants that perform best in coarse, well-drained soil. They are extremely drought tolerant and are resistant to insect pests and disease. Established plants require little or no summer water where the climate is moderated by the ocean. Some water may be needed, however, in hot interior valleys and in the desert. Maintenance requirements for wrinkleleaf rockrose are minimal. Sageleaf rockrose tends to be a little rank: Tip-pruning will keep the plant compact and encourage prostrate growth. Although rockroses are sturdy, withstanding drying winds, heat, and salt spray, they have limited cold tolerance. They are best suited to western gardens and will not survive in northern regions or in the southeastern United States. They do not tolerate humidity.

Uses Both of these rockroses are excellent large-scale ground covers for steep slopes and areas where water and maintenance cannot be provided. They have deep, extensive root systems that control erosion. They are also valuable for landscaping to reduce the fire hazard around homes in brush areas. They are effective in rock gardens and as informal borders where there is no foot traffic.

Convallaria
Lily-of-the-valley

Hardy to zone 3 (-40° F)

Convallaria majalis (lily-of-the-valley) is one of the hardiest and most adaptable ground covers. It thrives in partial or full shade and develops a dense mass of soil-holding roots. Leaves die back in fall and are renewed in spring. New leaves grow to 8 inches long and 1 to 3 inches wide. The fragrant, ¼-inch-wide, usually white bell-shaped flowers appear in spring. Available cultivars include 'Fortin's Giant', which has larger flowers than the species; *C. majalis* var. *rosea,* with pale pink flowers; and 'Flore Pleno', with double white flowers. The leaves of 'Striata' have thin white stripes.

Culture Lilies-of-the-valley grow in just about any soil but do not thrive or bloom well in mild-winter climates. They are subject to fungal blight, which can wipe out entire colonies. However, when planted on 7-inch centers where conditions are favorable, they spread to create a ground cover that needs almost no attention. Divide the clumps anytime.

Uses Lilies-of-the-valley are deciduous, best planted where the lack of winter foliage won't be a problem. They are used typically around shrubs, such as the taller rhododendrons and camellias, and also are effective with ferns.

Coprosma
Coprosma

Hardy to zone 9 (20° F)

Two species of *Coprosma* grow as ground covers, exclusively on the West Coast. *C. kirkii* is a sturdy, evergreen shrub with woody, upright, heavily branched stems of yellow-green. The oblong leaves are ¾ inch long. *C. kirkii* grows to 1½ to 2½ feet at a moderate rate. *C. pumila* is lower growing, with broadly oval, lustrous bright green leaves. 'Verde Vista' is a superior variety. Both species have inconspicuous flowers.

Culture These are drought-resistant plants that adapt to a wide range of soils. Keep them dense and at the desired

Cornus canadensis (bunchberry)

Coronilla varia (crown vetch)

height with 2 prunings a year. Plant in sun or partial shade—they do best in some shade except in foggy areas. Plant 2 feet apart.

Uses   Coprosmas are useful in an informal setting planted against a fence or pruned as a low hedge. They are best used as a small-scale ground cover on a slope or bank near the beach, where they can withstand wind and spray.

Cornus
Dogwood

Hardy to zone 5 (-20° F)

Cornus canadensis (bunchberry), a relative of the well-known dogwood tree, is useful as a ground cover. Bunchberry is native from Alaska to New Mexico to West Virginia, growing in cool, moist, acidic soil. In open woodlands it can be found covering areas up to a mile square. It spreads (not invasively) by underground runners and rarely grows taller than 9 inches. Tiny flower clusters appear in early spring and are surrounded by pure white bracts. Bright red

fruits mature by late summer. Leaves turn bright yellow to red in fall.

Culture   Bunchberries can be difficult to establish: Proper soil preparation is crucial. Soil should be loose and acidic. Work in lots of leaf mold, rotten bark, or pine needles. Transplant whole sods (if possible) in 5- or 6-square-foot sections. Plant in a site that is cool and moist but has plenty of springtime sun, such as under deciduous trees.

Uses   Once established, these are plants of rare beauty. Bunchberries do well in woodland and mountain gardens and as a ground cover around rhododendrons, azaleas, and similar plants.

Coronilla
Crown vetch

Hardy to zone 3 (-40° F)

The deep, soil-building roots and dense, weed-choking, 2-foot top growth of *Coronilla varia* (crown vetch) have made this one of the most popular ground covers for erosion control. However, it dies back in winter, and the mass

of brown stems can be a fire hazard in some areas. Leaves consist of many ½-inch-long oval leaflets. Pinkish flowers appear in summer.

Culture   Crown vetch can be planted by seed—use about 1 pound per 1,000 square feet. Transplant crowns (on 2-foot centers) or whole sods for more effective establishment. Crown vetch is drought resistant; it prefers full sun but tolerates some shade. It spreads by underground runners, so it can be invasive and difficult to eradicate. Mow in spring (using a sharp rotary or flail-type mower) for a beautiful green summer carpet.

Uses   Crown vetch is excellent for erosion control and for large areas that are difficult to maintain. Honeybees use the flowers.

Cotoneaster
Cotoneaster

Hardy to zone 5 (-20° F)

There are many cotoneasters suitable as ground covers. Among them are varieties adapted to virtually every climate of North America. Some

are deciduous; others are evergreen. Each produces attractive flowers in spring and berries in fall. All are deep rooted and good soil binders.

Cotoneaster horizontalis (rock cotoneaster) is perhaps the most widely grown of the cotoneasters. It is semi-evergreen in mild climates, losing leaves for only a short time; elsewhere it is deciduous. Bright red berries cover the branches during the winter months. Mass plantings maintain a 2- to 3-foot height. Branches eventually spread to 8 to 10 feet, sometimes more. Flowers and fruit are small; leaves are round, ½ inch in diameter, and become reddish before falling. Rock cotoneaster works well with low-growing junipers. It is especially effective on banks and in low dividers to discourage traffic. It is hardy to -20° F.

C. adpressus (creeping cotoneaster) is a deciduous type that eventually reaches 1½ feet high and spreads to 6 feet. Small, ¼-inch-diameter flowers are pink tinted; red fruits are the same size.

Cotoneaster horizontalis (rock cotoneaster)

Cotoneaster dammeri var. *radicans* (bearberry cotoneaster)

Leaves are small (½ inch long) and dark green. *C. a.* var. *praecox* is more vigorous and grows taller than the species (to 2 to 3 feet) and has slightly larger leaves and berries. *C. adpressus* is noted for its short, rigid branches and dense, low habit. It is hardy to -20° F.

C. apiculatus (cranberry cotoneaster) is similar to creeping cotoneaster. Cranberry cotoneaster has larger berries that remain on the plant throughout winter. It is deciduous, grows to 1 to 2 feet high, and spreads to 4 to 5 feet. Flowers are pinkish and appear in clusters; leaves are nearly round, usually less than ½ inch in diameter, and slightly hairy on the undersides. This species is also hardy to -20° F.

The smallest-leaved, finest-textured cotoneaster is *C. microphyllus* (rockspray, or small-leaved cotoneaster), an evergreen with trailing branches that spread to 6 feet; smaller branches grow upright to 2 to 3 feet. White flowers appear in June; scarlet berries mature in fall. Leaves are small, ¼ to ½ inch long, and shiny green on top. Fine hairs give the undersides of the leaves a grayish cast. 'Cochleatus' is smaller than the species. Leaves are spoon shaped and may have rolled edges. 'Thymifolius' is a very compact form with stiff, prostrate branches. 'Emerald Spray' is resistant to fire blight, a disease that often attacks cotoneasters.

The tangled, intermingling stems of rockspray are well suited for banks or around rocks. This cotoneaster must be thriving to look attractive—amend the soil before planting. Rockspray is hardy to -10° F.

C. congestus (Himalayan, or Pyrenees, cotoneaster) is a slow-growing evergreen. It reaches its maximum height (about 3 feet) and spread (3 feet) in roughly 5 years. Flowers are small, whitish pink, and appear in June. Berries are bright red. Leaves are similar to those of rockspray but are more rounded and do not have the fine hairs. The Himalayan cotoneaster is a rugged evergreen. Because of its slow growth rate, it is easy to care for once established. This species is hardy to -5° F.

C. conspicuus (necklace cotoneaster) is a very prostrate evergreen form. Secondary branches grow vertically to 1 to 1½ feet. Ultimate spread is 6 to 8 feet. Flowers are white; berries are fairly large, covering the branches in fall. Leaves are ¼ inch long and are dark green on top with paler undersides. Necklace cotoneaster is a good ground cover but is not dense enough to shade out weeds. It is hardy to 0° F.

C. dammeri (bearberry cotoneaster) spreads to 10 feet wide and reaches 2 to 3 feet in height at maturity. It is among the hardiest of the evergreen cotoneaster ground covers. Leaves are 1 inch long and oval shaped, glossy green above, and pale, sometimes whitish beneath. Flowers are white. There are many cultivars. 'Lowfast' is a fast grower with slightly smaller leaves more widely spaced on the branches. 'Royal Beauty' (sometimes called 'Coral Beauty' because of its coral-colored berries) and 'Skogholmen' are similarly vigorous and fast growing but are also noted for their springtime flower display. 'Eichholz' has carmine red fruits and some leaf color in fall; 'Major' is very similar but has slightly longer leaves. All are hardy to -20° F.

C. salicifolius (willowleaf cotoneaster) is distinguished by its 3½-inch-long, narrow leaves and scarlet fruits that persist into winter. It is evergreen to semievergreen. Cultivars include 'Herbstfeuer' ('Autumn Fire'), named for its leaves, which take on a reddish purple color in fall. 'Repens' has small, narrow, lustrous green leaves and abundant clusters of small fruit. 'Scarlet Leader', an upright, spreading form, grows 1 to 3 feet high and spreads to 6 feet.

Culture Cotoneasters are generally rugged and hardy plants. They are easy to grow, transplant, and care for. Many species thrive even in heavy clay soil. Plant cotoneasters in sun to partial shade. Prune them to shape—do not shear. Watch for pest damage, especially scale, red spider mite,

Cyrtomium falcatum (Japanese holly fern)

Cytisus decumbens (prostrate broom)

and lace bugs; check with a local nursery for the best means of control. Fire blight, a bacterial disease, attacks cotoneasters and is devastating in the East and the South. Leaves suddenly wilt on an infected twig, turn brown, but don't fall off. Prune out diseased branches and disinfect pruning tools after use with a 5 percent bleach solution.

Uses   Although use varies somewhat by species, cotoneasters make excellent ground covers in a variety of settings. Plant them to cover banks, drape over rocks, or trail along walls.

Cotula
New Zealand brass buttons

Hardy to zone 7 (0° F)

Cotula squalida (recently reclassified as *Leptinella squalida*) is an evergreen perennial with delicate, fernlike foliage and small, dull greenish yellow flower heads that look like brass buttons and are produced heavily during the summer. Individual leaves are finely divided, bronze green in color, and cov-

ered with soft hairs. The plant grows 2 to 3 inches high and creeps along the ground for a foot or more. The creeping stems root along their length to form a thick, dense carpet, making this plant a valuable lawn substitute.

Culture   This plant grows best in a moist, rich soil and in full sun to light shade. In areas where temperatures drop to 0° F, the foliage dies back for a time but recovers quickly when warm weather returns. Propagate by division in spring; space new plants 4 to 6 inches apart.

Uses   This species is tough and can withstand considerable traffic. It makes an unusual, attractive alternative to grass or dichondra (page 70) for small-scale lawns. It also can be used effectively as a ground cover between stepping-stones and in rock gardens.

Cyrtomium
Holly fern

Hardy to zone 9 (20° F)

A common houseplant, *Cyrtomium falcatum* (Japanese

holly fern) makes a handsome, dense ground cover outdoors in mild climates. Leaves are shiny, leathery, and light yellowish green. Fronds are about 2½ feet long with leaflets about 3 inches long.

Culture   Holly ferns tolerate drier air and more sun than many ferns but prefer a rich, moist soil. Spaced on 1½-foot centers, they grow together to form a solid cover. Do not plant them too deep or crowns may rot. Hose off dusty leaves and watch for brown scale.

Uses   These plants are effective bordering walks and paths. Grow them under camellias and other similar tall, evergreen shrubs.

Cytisus
Broom

Hardy to zone 5 (-20° F)

Ground cover brooms include members of two genera, *Cytisus* and *Genista* (see page 76). Some varieties have naturalized on both the Atlantic and Pacific coasts and are particularly visible in early spring when they are covered

with yellow flowers like those of sweet peas.

One of the most useful low-growing brooms is *C.* × *kewensis* (Kew broom). It grows only 6 to 10 inches high but spreads 3 feet. The trailing branches are handsome cascading over low walls. Leaves are tiny and usually divided into 3 leaflets. Pale yellow, ½-inch flowers appear in May. *C. decumbens* (prostrate broom) differs only slightly from the Kew broom: Its flowers are bright yellow and bloom a few weeks later.

Culture   Brooms are very adaptable plants. Generally they do best in dry, poor, slightly acidic soil. If drainage is good, plentiful water is accepted. (Such is the case in the Northwest, where brooms thrive.) The greatest difficulty in growing brooms is getting them started or transplanted. Begin with young, cutting-grown plants in flats or containers. Once established, they require little or no care. Hardwood or softwood cuttings taken in August root best. Little pruning is necessary, but if plants become spindly, cut

Daphne cneorum (garland daphne)

Dianthus plumarius (Scotch pink)

them back after flowering. Kew broom is hardy to -5° F; prostrate broom is hardy to -20° F.

Uses These are excellent plants for hot, dry, sunny locations. In the Southwest, they combine well with many of the drought-tolerant natives. Brooms are also good coastal plants: They tolerate salt-laden air and do well in sandy soil.

Daboecia
Irish heath

See *Erica*, page 71.

Daphne
Daphne

Hardy to zone 4 (-30° F)

Daphne cneorum (garland daphne) is a lovely, low evergreen shrub with 1-inch-long, glossy leaves. Fragrant pink flowers cover the plant in spring and sometimes again in late summer or fall. This plant grows slowly, mounding to 1 foot tall and twice as wide. 'Variegata' has dainty leaves edged with cream. 'Pygmaea'

has prostrate branches and abundant flowers. 'Ruby Glow' has deeper green leaves and darker pink flowers than the species. It spreads slowly to 3 feet.

D. collina (rose daphne), also a mounding evergreen, reaches 2 feet high and equally wide. Leaves are small and dark green; fragrant flowers of deep rose appear in April or May, sometimes again in fall. Rose daphne is grown mostly on the West Coast. *D. odora* (winter daphne) is widely planted, often in masses, in the Southeast. It grows to about 4 feet high (sometimes higher) and spreads to 5 feet or so. Leaves are narrow, thick, glossy, and about 3 inches long. Pink to deep red flowers appear in clusters at the ends of branches in late winter. Winter daphne is hardy in zones 7 to 9.

Culture Daphnes do best in full sun and in sandy, humus-enriched soil that is slightly acid. Mulch to keep roots cool. Buy plants in containers (seedlings are difficult to transplant). Water sparingly. Do

not prune back or disturb roots. Propagate from cuttings.

Uses These plants are used as accents in borders or for low edging. They are lovely interplanted with spring bulbs or in front of taller evergreens.

Dianthus
Pinks

Hardy to zone 2 (-50° F)

There are at least a hundred species and many more hybrids of pinks. Almost all have a spicy, usually clovelike scent and single or double flowers that are 1½ to 3 inches across. Flower color varies from white to pink to deep red. Cold tolerance differs as well. *Dianthus plumarius* (grass, cottage, or Scotch pink) is a relatively low-growing perennial that blooms from late May through summer. It has small, single or double flowers on stems rising 15 inches above a grasslike turf made of 3-inch-long, needle-tipped leaves. This species is hardy to -10° F.

D. deltoides (maiden pink), one of the most common pinks, makes a carpet of blue-green grasslike leaves. It

grows to 6 inches but can be kept to 2 to 3 inches by mowing. It blooms in June and is very hardy, to -50° F. *D. arenarius* (sandy pink) grows taller than maiden pink and is slightly less hardy (to -40° F). Its height, unmowed, reaches 8 to 9 inches. This species will tolerate some shade.

Culture Pinks are best started from seeds, but can also be grown from cuttings or by division. Space new plants 10 to 12 inches apart. They need full sun, a light soil (preferably with some lime), and good drainage. Mow after flowering to maintain even, compact growth and to remove spent blooms.

Uses Pinks are classic edging and rock garden plants.

Dicentra
Bleeding-heart

Hardy to zone 4 (-30° F)

Dicentra eximia (fringed bleeding-heart), native to the Northeast and southern mountain regions, is an easily grown perennial, well suited to shady corners. Not a ground cover for large areas, it forms

Dichondra micrantha (dichondra)

Dicentra eximia 'Alba' (fringed bleeding-heart)

Dryopteris goldiana (wood fern)

2-foot clumps 1 to 2 feet high (higher in shade). The heart-shaped pink flowers are carried on 12-inch spikes; they first appear in May and sporadically thereafter until frost. Leaves are fernlike and blue or gray-green. Of the many cultivars available, 'Bountiful' is one of the best, with darker green foliage and rich pink flowers.

D. formosa is native to the West. It is similar to *D. eximia* but spreads runners freely. 'Zestful' has an especially long blooming season; 'Luxuriant' has cherry pink flowers from late April and intermittently until October. These are borne on 18-inch stalks above ferny foliage. 'Snowdrift' forms a smaller clump than the species (about a foot wide) and has white flowers from spring to frost, carried on stalks 10 to 12 inches high.

Culture   Most well-drained soils are acceptable, but a rich humus is best. Shade is advisable unless the soil is unusually moist. To achieve a solid cover, plant clumps about 8 inches apart. Propagate by

seeds or division in early spring. Seedlings sometimes sprout nearby—these plants readily self-sow.

Uses   These are the perfect plants for turning that shady, unused corner into a place of beauty. Bleeding-hearts combine well with ferns and wildflowers. Use the cut foliage and flowers indoors for long-lasting arrangements.

Dichondra
Dichondra

Hardy to zone 8 (15° F)

Dichondra micrantha (formerly known as *D. repens*) is a prostrate, herbaceous perennial that comes as close to duplicating the ornamental functions of grass as any lawn substitute can—in those areas where it can be grown. Dichondra turf is formed by masses of cupped, horseshoe-shaped dark green leaves that are ¼ to ¾ inch across. They grow atop delicate stems averaging 1 to 3 inches in height. The plant spreads at a moderate rate by surface runners that develop roots.

Culture   Dichondra grows in sun or light shade and in heavy or light soil. Keep the soil evenly moist but never soggy. In hot, dry areas and in fast-draining soil, water daily; in cool, humid areas and in heavy soil, less frequent watering will suffice. Dichondra is commonly grown from sod, seeds, or by plugs. In all cases, prepare the soil carefully—as for a grass lawn. Sow seeds at the rate of 1 pound per 1,000 square feet. Establishment will take about 2 months. A flat of dichondra cut into 3-inch-square plugs will provide fast or slow cover depending on how far apart the plugs are spaced.

As with fine grass lawns, dichondra requires regular fertilizing during the active growing season. Water well after fertilizing to avoid burning the leaves. Control weeds and invading grasses, such as bermudagrass and crabgrass. Dichondra is not hardy, although it might survive brief exposure to temperatures as low as 15° F. Don't walk on frozen dichondra; any footprints will remain as dead spots. Watch for evidence of

fungal diseases—large brown spots on leaves. Dichondra flea beetle may also be a problem. Check with local nursery staffers for effective controls.

Uses   Where water use is not limited, dichondra makes a beautiful lawn substitute. Its chief advantage over grass is that it rarely needs to be mowed. However, it takes only the lightest traffic and is less resistant to weed invasion than most grasses.

Dryopteris
Wood fern, shield fern

Hardy to zone 3 (-35° F)

Dryopteris is a large group of ferns that includes many natives of forests in the United States and Canada. Most are very hardy, evergreen, and easy to grow. *D. austriaca* var. *spinulosa* (florist's fern) is widely distributed throughout eastern North America. Its fronds are harvested in summer and shipped in winter. It is hardy to -35° F. *D. marginalis* (leather wood fern), also native to the Northeast, grows in clumps to about 2 feet and is hardy to -35° F. *D. arguta*

Duchesnea indica (mock strawberry)

Epimedium (barrenwort)

(coastal wood fern) is native to western North America. It grows to about 3 feet and is hardy to 0° F.

Culture   All wood ferns need shade and a moist, humus-rich soil to thrive. Many forms spread by underground runners and thus are easily propagated by division.

Uses   These ferns are special-purpose ground covers, not used to cover large areas but to accent or complete a landscape. They are best in natural or native gardens.

Duchesnea
Mock strawberry, Indian-strawberry

Hardy to zone 4 (-30° F)

Duchesnea indica (mock strawberry) bears a superficial resemblance to *Fragaria chiloensis* (wild strawberry, page 74) but differs in several significant respects. Its leaves are thinner and smaller, and its flowers are yellow. It spreads rapidly by runners, like the wild strawberry, and

forms an equally dense but somewhat lower mat.

Culture   Cultural requirements for mock strawberry are the same as for wild strawberry with one important difference: Mock strawberry does best in light shade. It is also much hardier and can be invasive.

Uses   Mock strawberry is most attractive as a mass planting among a small grouping of trees or, in smaller areas, in the filtered shade of shrubs.

Epimedium
Barrenwort, bishop's-hat, epimedium

Hardy to zone 3 (-40° F)

The barrenworts are easy to grow, hardy, and too little used. They spread with creeping roots to make a 6- to 18-inch-high cover. The plant is semievergreen: Most of the leathery, heart-shaped leaves die back in winter, but a few last into January. In early spring the new leaves are pale green with some rose. During midseason, they are deep, glossy green; in fall, they are

reddish. Tiny, ½-inch, orchid-like flowers (shaped like a bishop's hat) appear in May. Many colors are available, and the flowers last well when cut.

Epimedium grandiflorum is the most commonly cultivated form. It grows to about 1 foot. Different cultivars offer different flower colors. 'Rose Queen' has bright, rosy flowers with white-tipped spurs. *E. × versicolor* 'Sulphureum' has yellow flowers. *E. × youngianum* 'Niveum' grows compactly and has white flowers.

Culture   These long-lived, easy-to-grow perennials are one of the most shade-tolerant ground covers. They do best in acidic soil that is rich and moist. The creeping roots are close to the surface; don't cultivate around them. Placed 10 inches apart, the plants will fill in without overcrowding. To propagate, divide the clumps in early spring. Cut off old leaves so that small flowers and new leaves will be visible.

Uses   Barrenworts thrive in the shade of other acid-soil

plants, such as the taller rhododendrons, camellias, and ferns. Their roots compete well with tree roots, so plant them around trees such as crab-apple and magnolia.

Erica
Heath

Hardy to zone 6 (-10° F)

Heaths are special plants loved by many collectors. They are finely textured with small, bell-shaped red to white flowers. Many varieties are available, including some that will bloom the year around in mild climates.

In mild-winter areas, *Erica herbacea* (spring, or Christmas, heath) begins blooming as early as November. Flowers appear in spring where winters are more severe. Spring heath makes an excellent ground cover, requiring little care once established. It is low growing, rarely exceeding 1 foot, and spreads to 2 to 3 feet (plant on 2½-foot centers). The evergreen leaves are less than ¼ inch long and circle the stem in groups of four. Flowers

Erica carnea (heath)

Erodium reichardii (cranesbill)

hang and are 1 to 2 inches long. In cold climates, some winter protection may be necessary. *E. vagans* (Cornish heath) is bushier and more rounded than spring heath. It is noted for its bright green leaves, purplish pink flowers, and hardiness.

Other plants are included in the general category of heaths. The *Daboecia* genus is composed of evergreen, heath-like shrubs that are grown and used in much the same manner as those of the *Erica* genus. *D. cantabrica* (Irish heath) is an 18-inch-tall shrub that carries slightly drooping, ½-inch-long lavender flowers on upright stems. Blooming begins in February in some areas, as late as May in others, continues throughout summer, and lasts as late as November. The leaves are most similar to Scotch heather (*Calluna*, page 61) but are smaller. Several different flower colors are available: Those of 'Alba' are white; of 'Praegerae', rose pink. Propagate by cuttings or division.

Culture　Heaths are tough, low-maintenance plants. They

do best in acidic soil but tolerate slight alkalinity. Soil must be moist and especially well drained. In dry or water-logged areas, add generous amounts of organic matter to the soil. Planting in raised beds or mounds also improves drainage. Heaths stay more compact and flower better in soils that are not too rich. Plant in partial (afternoon) shade in hot-summer areas. Roots are close to the surface, so instead of using a cultivator, apply a mulch to keep the soil loose. In early spring, cut back to remove flower stalks and to stimulate dense growth. Propagate by layering (see page 39).

Uses　The low-growing heaths serve very well not only as ground covers but also as borders and edging plants. Their root systems help prevent soil erosion on banks and slopes. They tolerate salt-laden coastal air and exposed, windy locations. The flowers dry and last many months indoors. Heaths are excellent low-maintenance ground covers, requiring almost no attention once established.

Erodium
Cranesbill, heronsbill

Hardy to zone 8 (20° F)

Erodium reichardii (cranesbill) has dense, delicately textured green foliage that grows in clumps 3 to 6 inches high, spreads slowly to about 1 foot, and turns reddish in winter. Leaves are small, lightly lobed, and ovate. White, pink-veined, ½-inch-wide flowers bloom from spring through summer. This species gets its popular names from the ½-inch-long, needlelike stalks seen at the stem ends after the flowers fall off. *E. r.* 'Roseum' has pink flowers veined with red.

Culture　Cranesbill is an adaptable plant but does best in shade, in soil with good drainage. Water enough to keep the plant moist. It is easily propagated by seeds or division; set plants 6 inches apart for quick coverage.

Uses　Cranesbill is excellent in rock gardens and as a small-scale ground cover. It can't take any traffic.

Euonymus
Wintercreeper

Hardy to zone 4 (-25° F)

Euonymus fortunei (wintercreeper) is an evergreen vine or shrub that makes a very useful ground cover. When used as a shrub, its branches trail and sometimes root. Pointed, somewhat leathery, jagged dark green leaves, 1½ to 2 inches long, are set opposite one another along trailing stems. Flowers are only occasionally produced and are inconspicuous. The plant spreads rapidly to about 4 feet while building up to a height of about 2 feet.

Several cultivars make better ground covers than the species. The most widely used is *E. f.* 'Colorata' (purpleleaf wintercreeper), characterized by the striking purple color of its foliage in fall and winter. It forms a fairly dense carpet 6 to 10 inches high and responds well to mowing. *E. f.* 'Kewensis' and *E. f.* 'Minima' (baby wintercreeper) are dwarf types that are more delicate and slower and lower growing, reaching a height of hardly more than 2 inches. Both

Euonymus fortunei 'Emerald 'n Gold' (wintercreeper)

Forsythia viridissima 'Bronxensis' (greenstem forsythia)

Festuca glauca (blue fescue)

retain their small, evergreen leaves throughout the year. (The leaves of 'Minima' are somewhat larger than those of 'Kewensis'.) *E. f.* 'Gracilis' (variegated wintercreeper) is smaller and less vigorous than 'Colorata'. Variegated whitish leaves that take on a pink tinge in winter distinguish this cultivar. *E. f.* 'Gracilis' is the fastest growing of the small-leaved varieties.

E. f. 'Emerald Cushion', also small leaved, is a mounding cultivar with compact branches and rich green foliage. 'Emerald Leader' and 'Emerald Beauty', both with beautiful fruit, spread 5 to 6 feet and can reach 6 feet in height. 'Emerald 'n Gold' stays low and compact (1½ to 2 feet tall). The dark green leaves have yellow edges and turn pink-red in winter. 'Emerald Surprise' is an upright shrub. Leaves are variegated with green, gold, and creamy white. 'Emerald Gaiety', a widely planted cultivar, has leaves with cream-colored margins.

Culture Wintercreepers are hardy, sturdy plants that grow in most parts of the United States and southern Canada, in sun or shade, and in good or poor soil. They are drought resistant but do not do well in hot, desert areas even when adequately watered. Propagate by division, layering, or cuttings. Plant divided or rooted plants in spring and set about 2 feet apart. Wintercreepers are particularly subject to scale infestation. This causes yellowish or whitish spots on the leaves; later, leaves drop and branches die. Control scale with a dormant oil spray in early spring.

Uses The dwarf and other small-leaved varieties are highly effective trailing over walls and between rocks and stepping-stones. Plant the larger forms, including purpleleaf wintercreeper in masses, on steep hillsides (where they provide good erosion control), or wherever they might serve to cover barren, unsightly areas.

Festuca
Fescue

Hardy to zone 3 (-40° F)

Festuca glauca (blue fescue) is an attractive ornamental grass composed of hairlike leaves growing 4 to 10 inches high in rounded bluish gray tufts. Although a true grass, it is not a practical lawn substitute because of its mounding growth habit.

Culture Grow blue fescue in ordinary, well-drained soil and full sun. It is drought resistant but does need regular summer watering. Apply a light mulch to minimize weed growth between tufts. Mow in early spring before growth starts. Clip shabby plants to remove seed heads, restore appearance, and stimulate new growth. Start new plants from divisions.

Uses When planted in larger areas, blue fescue looks best in geometric patterns rather than at random. Two or three plants can provide a nice accent; a row makes a good walkway border or edging for a flower bed. Blue fescue can also be used effectively as a filler in perennial borders.

Forsythia
Forsythia

Hardy to zone 5 (-15° F)

Among the forsythias are several suitable as ground covers. *Forsythia viridissima* (greenstem forsythia) has deep green foliage, olive green stems, and greenish yellow flowers. *F. v.* 'Bronxensis' bears yellow flowers in early spring on dense branches that grow only 12 inches tall (considerably smaller than the species) and spreads quickly in flat-topped mounds from 2 to 3 feet wide. *F.* × *intermedia* 'Arnold Dwarf' grows 2 to 3 feet high and spreads to 6 to 7 feet; its stems root wherever they touch the soil. The greenish yellow flowers are sparse and not showy.

Culture These plants do best in acid soil. They tolerate a little shade but prefer sun. Prune after bloom—remove the older branches and any weakened or dead wood.

Uses These forsythias are common ground covers in the East and Midwest. They provide excellent erosion control on banks and work very well in mass plantings.

Fragaria chiloensis (wild strawberry)

Galium odoratum (sweet woodruff)

Gaultheria procumbens (teaberry, checkerberry)

Fragaria

Wild strawberry, sand strawberry

Hardy to zone 5 (-15° F)

An ancestor of all commercial strawberries, the evergreen *Fragaria chiloensis* (wild strawberry) forms a thick mat of 2-inch-wide dark green leaves that turn a reddish hue in winter. Leaves are oval, roughly toothed on their upper parts, crinkly textured, and glossy. A profusion of 1-inch-wide white flowers appears in spring, followed by small, edible, but not too tasty fruit. Hybrid Ornamental Strawberry Number 25, developed and tested in southern California, is similar to the species but grows more vigorously, is larger in all respects, and produces delicious fruit.

Culture Wild strawberry grows best in full sun and in most well-drained soils; it does particularly well in sand dunes at the beach. Water regularly throughout the year. Stimulate foliage growth with light mowing in spring. Start new plants from sections of runners planted 12 inches apart. Watch for red spider mite infestations; control by spraying twice a year with a combination spray.

Uses Use wild strawberry anywhere in the garden, in beds, or as borders. It contributes a delightful, woodsy effect. It is an ideal ground cover for beachlike conditions and is particularly useful on slopes. Wild strawberry accepts light traffic.

Galium

Sweet woodruff

Hardy to zone 4 (-30° F)

Galium odoratum (sweet woodruff) is a beautiful ground cover for shady spots. It grows rapidly, spreading by underground stems, to become a dense mat. Tiny white flowers in the shape of 4-petal crosses last from April into summer. They appear in clusters at the end of slender stems, 6 to 12 inches high, that are covered by long, narrow leaves set in whorls of 8. The leaves have a delicate fragrance suggestive of fresh hay or vanilla.

Culture This perennial herb does best in partial or full shade and moist, loamy soil. It will not do well in humid climates. Propagate by dividing the creeping stems at the beginning of the dormant winter period. In spring, set out new plants 8 to 12 inches apart. Sweet woodruff self-sows freely once established.

Uses This plant provides a lovely effect under trees, well-developed rose bushes, and rhododendrons, and along shady garden paths. It is also a good bulb cover. Dried leaves are used in sachets, as a tea, and to flavor wine drinks. Sweet woodruff is too delicate for traffic.

Gardenia

Gardenia

Hardy to zone 8 (15° F)

Gardenia augusta 'Radicans' (creeping gardenia) is a low and slow-growing evergreen form of the common gardenia. It reaches 12 inches in height and spreads 2 to 3 feet. The fragrant white flowers appear in early summer and are about 1 inch in diameter. Leaves are glossy green.

Culture Like the common gardenia, the lower-growing forms do best in moist, acidic, well-drained soil. Use an organic mulch and replenish it regularly. All gardenias need lots of high summer heat. Plant them in some shade, although full sun is tolerated. Prune upright-growing branches to stimulate horizontal growth.

Uses Creeping gardenia is an excellent small-scale ground cover and a good container plant.

Gaultheria

Wintergreen

Hardy to zone 3 (-40° F)

Gaultheria procumbens, also called teaberry or checkerberry, is a beautiful, herblike, evergreen woody plant with stems rising only 2 to 6 inches. The round leaves become leathery with age and turn a rich burgundy in fall and winter. They contain wintergreen, an aromatic oil. Flowers are small, nodding white bells and

Gazania (gazania)

Gaylussacia brachycera (box huckleberry)

Gelsemium sempervirens var. *rankinii* (Carolina jessamine)

are followed by edible, pulpy red berries that become mealy and pink with age. Berries not eaten by chipmunks, grouse, mice, or birds may remain until spring. 'Macrocarpa' is a compact, improved cultivar that has quantities of flowers and fruits.

Culture Plant wintergreen in partial shade and moist, acid soil rich in humus. Set plants 12 inches apart. These plants spread 4 to 6 inches in a year by underground stems. To propagate, take stem cuttings in early summer. Wintergreen does not do well in desert areas.

Uses These plants are often used under trees and shrubs, in open woodlands, or along edges of timber. They also do well cascading over walls, rocks, or banks.

Gaylussacia
Box huckleberry

Hardy to zone 5 (to -20° F)

Gaylussacia brachycera (box huckleberry) is a low-growing evergreen shrub, 8 to 18 inches tall, and attractive the year around. Leaves are

smooth and elliptic, ⅛ to 1 inch long, and crimson when young. Small, bell-shaped flowers hang in little bunches and open to a soft pink or white. Stems are red. Fruits are edible and resemble blueberries but without as fine a flavor.

Culture Box huckleberry grows best in moist, acid soil, in partial shade. Propagate from cuttings or by dividing the creeping roots and branches.

Uses This plant is useful under trees and shrubs (especially pines and rhododendrons), as an edging plant in shrub borders, or as a cover in small, hard-to-mow areas.

Gazania
Gazania

Hardy to zone 8 (15° F)

This perennial ground cover is widely used in California and the Southwest. (It is subject to root rot in the Southeast.) Foliage is typically grayish, fairly dense, and reaches a height of 2½ to 6 inches. Flowers come in a variety of colors,

including white, pink, yellow, and bronze. Plants bloom from late spring through summer and intermittently throughout the rest of the year. The flowers of 'Sun Gold' are deep yellow at the center, lighter yellow at the tips; 'Sunburst' has yellow flowers with orange tips.

Culture Gazanias grow best in moist soils that have good drainage. Plant them in a warm, sunny location, and water 2 or 3 times a month in hot weather. Propagate by dividing plants in spring.

Uses Gazanias are effective as specimen plants and in mass plantings. They are also useful on slopes and in parking lots and median strips as borders.

Gelsemium
Carolina jessamine

Hardy to zone 7 (0° F)

Gelsemium sempervirens (Carolina jessamine) is widely used in gardens in the Deep South, as far north as Virginia. It is a semievergreen to evergreen plant, losing its leaves

in areas where winters are especially cold. Leaves are shiny green and finely textured. This plant is most appreciated for its fragrant flowers, which are yellow, tubular, and about 1 inch long. Plants bloom in early spring. 'Plena', also called 'Pride of Augusta', is a lovely, vigorous cultivar with double yellow flowers that are more abundant and continue over a longer time than the single form. *G. s.* var. *rankinii* blooms in spring and fall—the flowers have no fragrance.

Culture This plant tolerates some shade but flowers more profusely in full sun. Prune selectively and frequently to keep it low (about 3 feet) and to encourage new growth from the base. Almost any soil is suitable, but the plant grows best in good loam. Propagate by seeds, or for 'Plena' by cuttings.

Uses Carolina jessamine is best used as a cover for large areas. It looks attractive on a bank or spilling over a retaining wall.

Genista lydia (common woodwaxen, dyers greenwood)

Hedera helix (English ivy)

Genista
Broom

Hardy to zone 5 (-20° F)

This group of shrubs is so closely related to *Cytisus* (page 68) that the two are difficult to distinguish. *Genista,* like *Cytisus,* is adapted to dry-summer Mediterranean climates and is therefore an excellent plant for poor and dry soils. *Genista pilosa* (silky-leaf woodwaxen) is one of the best low-growing brooms. It is deciduous, with leaves about ½ inch long. In winter the bare twigs remain green. The plant spreads to form a clump up to 7 feet wide and 1 to 1½ feet high. Sweetpea-like yellow flowers appear in May. This species tolerates temperatures to -10° F.

G. sagittalis (arrow broom) is among the hardiest of the brooms (to -20° F). Branches are bright green in winter; flowers appear in June. Height and spread are similar to *G. pilosa. G. tinctoria,* another of the hardy brooms, is small to medium in height. It has the characteristic yellow flowers in summer and green branches

in winter. *G. lydia* (common woodwaxen or dyers greenwood) reaches 1 to 2 feet in height and spreads 1 to 4 feet. It is a less hardy broom, useful in zones 6 to 9, except in the desert. Slender, arching branches are covered in early summer with golden yellow flowers.

Culture These are plants for hot, dry, sunny locations. They require little maintenance and are exceptionally tolerant once established, but can be difficult to transplant. Propagate by cuttings taken in August. See *Cytisus,* page 68, for more information.

Uses The brooms are useful along banks and at the seaside. They blend quietly into the landscape most of the year except for springtime, when their flowers provide an eye-catching display.

Hedera
Ivy

Hardy to zone 5 (-20° F)

Ivy, well known and widely used, is an adaptable, dependable evergreen ground cover. It grows rapidly in sun

to deep shade. Leaves vary from bright to hunter green and have definite stems. Young foliage has the characteristic lobed heart shape. Ivy stays within 2 to 12 inches of the ground unless it has access to something to climb. Clinging with aerial rootlets, it can reach as high as 90 feet. Only high in trees does it develop its mature, diamond-shaped leaves, fall-blooming flowers, and dark berrylike fruit.

There are three main species of ivy; *Hedera helix* (English ivy) is the most common. It is hardy in zones 5 to 9, depending on the cultivar. Leaves are mostly 3 to 5 lobed and 2 to 4 inches long. Like all the ivies, this species transplants easily, grows vigorously, and competes well with tree roots. There are many cultivars, some of which are sold under several different names. (Ivy tends to "throw sports." This refers to the spontaneous changes that occur in the plant's genetic makeup that result in leaves that may differ from the original in color, size, shape, or arrangement. Hence the

confusing array of cultivars.) In general, the larger-leaved varieties tend to be extra hardy; the dwarf, small-leaved kinds are more tender.

Some of the best cultivars are 'Angularis Aurea', with bright green leaves partly suffused with deep yellow; 'Anna Marie', with light, almost gray-green leaves daintily edged in white; 'Baltica', one of the most popular varieties, with small dark green leaves veined in white; 'Buttercup', with light green leaves in shade, some leaves of green-yellow in the sun, others completely yellow; and 'Hibernica', with large, lustrous leaves. 'Thorndale' is hardy, with leaves larger than the species; 'Bulgaria' is one of the hardiest of the English ivies.

Within *H. helix* are also some more classic varieties. 'Deltoidea' has heart-shaped dark green dull leaves with 3 rounded lobes and gray-green veins. It has purple tones in fall and winter. The leaves of 'Fluffy Ruffles' curl at the edges and appear rounded. They have 5 lobes and are a midgreen strongly veined in yellow-green. 'Green Feather'

Hedera helix 'Buttercup' (English ivy)

Hedera colchica (Colchis, or Persian, ivy)

is compact growing and has bird's-foot-shaped leaves. The leaves of 'Gold Heart' have green margins and white centers. 'Hibernica Variegata' leaves may have butter yellow edges, markings, or suffusion; some may be entirely yellow, others all green. 'Ivalace' is a unique cultivar, with cupped medium green leaves whose veins, undersides, and frilly edges are a lighter green. 'Minor Marmorata' has dark green leaves frosted with white. 'Sagittifolia Variegata' has mottled gray and dark green leaves finely edged in white. Most are 3 lobed with a long, slender center lobe like a bird's foot. 'Triton' has bright deep green leaves with prominent veins that are otherwise quite unusual: The 3 center lobes are long, wispy, and twisted to fine points.

H. colchica (Colchis, or Persian, ivy) has slightly larger, lustrous, heart-shaped leaves and a coarser texture than English ivy. It is hardy in zones 6 to 9 and is grown from Philadelphia south. This is a very fast growing species. It grows well in shade but tol-

erates full sun and dry soil. 'Dentata' has rich pea green young leaves. These turn dark green as they mature and range in size from 5 to 10 inches. Leaf margins have widely spaced fine teeth; veins are light green and relatively inconspicuous. The leaves of 'Dentata Variegata' have deep cream yellow edges and dark green centers marbled with gray-green. Some leaves are almost entirely yellow-white. 'Sulphur Heart' reverses the 'Dentata Variegata' pattern— leaf veins and centers are creamy yellow or light green.

H. canariensis (Algerian ivy), native to the Canary Islands and the area surrounding the Mediterranean sea, is hardy only in zones 9 and 10. Its 3- to 5-lobed leaves grow up to 8 inches across, but most are about half that size. New leaves are light green; older growth is dark and glossy. This makes an appealing contrast. Stems are burgundy red. Like other ivies, this species roots as it spreads. It is more aggressive than the others, however, and requires more moisture. Algerian ivy forms a ground-hugging mat that can

extend to 12 inches in height. Since it is rather rampant, it is better for large areas than for small gardens. In addition, its coarser texture looks best at a distance.

H. canariensis 'Gloire-de-Marengo', a useful ground cover for large areas, is sometimes used along California freeways. Leaves have creamy white edges; centers are marbled with dark and silver green. (New leaves are almost more white than green.) 'Margine-maculata' has lighter green leaves dusted with yellowish white, with light yellowish edges. These two cultivars are likely to start in one form and then mutate to the other. 'Ravensholst' has glossy dark green leaves with lighter veins. The leaves of 'Variegata' are edged in yellowish white.

Culture Plant ivies in well-drained, rich, fairly moist soil. Space English ivy plants 12 inches apart, Algerian and Persian ivy plants 18 inches apart. Ivies grow best in indirect light, but, once established, some kinds will tolerate full sun if kept watered. (Al-

gerian ivy is better for sunny locations.) Ivies also flourish in deep shade. Take cuttings anytime, but those taken after the growth spurts in spring and particularly in fall do best. Ivies root easily, even in water. For best transplants, take 2-node cuttings or stem sections (not necessarily stem ends) and set them shallowly in a rooting medium (see page 39). Keep them moist and place in indirect light until roots appear.

English ivy is more drought tolerant than Algerian ivy, but in hot, dry regions, all ivies require regular watering (see page 36). Do not over-water plants in shady areas where the soil does not dry out as often. In colder areas, apply an antitranspirant spray (available at nurseries) to limit water loss due to drying winter winds. Fertilize ivy plantings with high-nitrogen fertilizer in early spring and again in midsummer. Mow Persian and Algerian ivy every year, English ivy at least every other year, just prior to new growth, with the mower at the highest setting. Use a nylon string trimmer on slopes

Helianthemum nummularium 'Rose Queen' (sunrose)

Hemerocallis (daylily)

too steep for mowers. Mowing or trimming prevents the growth from becoming too dense. (A thick mat of ivy will harbor a variety of pests, including snails, slugs, and rats.) Mow Algerian ivy a second time (in July) where the growing season is long. This will stimulate more uniform and weed-free growth. Trim the edges of the ivy planting 2 to 4 times a year with hedge shears or a sharp spade, or control by mowing. Ivy will cover a path or darken a window if left untrimmed. Delayed trimming becomes more difficult, because uncut plants soon grow woody and tangled.

Watch ivies for leaf spot, which begins as ¼-inch-long brown or black spots. Generally this is not serious, but if spots become unsightly, spray the affected area with tribasic copper. To prevent the spread of disease, water in the morning when the foliage is cooler and so that the leaves are dry by nightfall.

Uses   Small-leaved ivies are excellent ground covers between bulbs. All ivies are useful under trees and around shrubs and taller ground covers. Ivy is famous for covering stone and brick buildings, but the clinging rootlets can damage painted surfaces if allowed to climb. Use ivy to turn wire or chain-link fences into green walls. Plant on slopes or banks to prevent erosion. Use ivy also as an attractive edging cascading over the sides of window boxes and large patio planters.

Helianthemum
Sunrose

Hardy to zone 5 (-20° F)

Helianthemum nummularium (sunrose) is a hardy, spreading, evergreen plant that makes an excellent, low-maintenance ground cover. As a vigorous, long-lived native of the Mediterranean region, it is adapted to dry summers. Its height is usually 6 to 8 inches, although some plants reach 1 foot. Each plant ultimately forms a clump about 3 feet in diameter. Branches root as they spread, eventually creating a thick mat. Leaves are narrow, growing to 1 inch in length, and are glossy or dull green, depending on the variety. Bright, 1- to 2-inch-wide flowers are single or double and come in shades of pink, red, and yellow. Individual blossoms are delicate and last only a day, but the plant flowers over a long period.

Culture   Sunroses need full sun and infertile, neutral-to-alkaline soil. Amend acid soils with lime before planting. These plants do best in dry soil and will not withstand high humidity. Shear sunroses in spring, after the first flowering, to stimulate growth and a late-summer bloom, and to keep the plants dense and compact. Transplanting can be difficult: Purchase rooted cuttings if possible and plant 12 to 18 inches apart. Sunroses do not tolerate root disturbances once they are established. Do not cultivate around them or transplant. Where winters are cold and there is no snow cover, insulate the plants with straw or similar material to protect them from drying winds. Propagate with cuttings from new spring growth (late June) or by division.

Uses   Sunroses do very well in rock gardens, either cascading over and around rocks or tucked into pockets. A close relative of the rockroses (*Cistus,* page 64), they also have fire-retardant properties.

Hemerocallis
Daylily

Hardy to zone 3 (-35° F)

Daylilies grow in almost any type of soil or climate and fit into the landscape in many ways. They are disease resistant, virtually pest free, and offer spectacular and fragrant flowers. A well-selected combination of varieties will produce flowers from May to October in the mildest climates, perhaps a month or so less in cold regions. Some daylilies are repeat bloomers; some bloom in the evening. Flowers are from 3 to 8 inches across; colors range from the original yellow, orange, rust, and red to hybrids in pink, vermilion, buff, apricot, white, and two-color varieties. Plants range in height from the 12-inch dwarfs up to 6 feet. There are both evergreen daylilies

Heuchera micrantha var. *diversifolia* 'Palace Purple' (coralbells)

Hosta fortunei 'Robusta' (plantain lily, funkia)

for warm climates and deciduous types that grow nearly anywhere.

Culture   Plant daylilies in spring, on 2-foot centers. Water before and during bloom to ensure the best flowering. Apply a balanced fertilizer in spring and early summer. Daylilies do best if divided every 4 to 6 years. Dig the entire clump in early spring (or late fall for deciduous varieties). Insert 2 spading forks into the center of the clump, then pull the handles in opposite directions to pry the clump into 2, 3, or 4 parts. Replant these divisions with the top of the fleshy roots at soil level.

Uses   The uses of daylilies are varied. Some, such as *Hemerocallis fulva* 'Europa', are so tough that they can reclaim poor or damaged soil, grow by railroad tracks, or hold riverbanks. Daylilies make excellent cut flowers. Choose a stem with several ready-to-bloom buds. In the house the buds will open, one per day, each lasting only a day. (Translated from the Greek, *hemerocallis* means *beautiful for the day.*)

Heuchera
Coralbells

Hardy to zone 3 (-35° F)

Heuchera sanguinea (coralbells) is an evergreen perennial popular throughout the United States. It is not a large-scale ground cover but is well suited for brightening small spots. The flowers are bell shaped, white, coral pink, or red, and about ½ inch long. They are borne on 14- to 24-inch-long stalks that appear first in spring and sporadically until September. In mild-winter areas, the plants may bloom all year. Evergreen leaves are roundish and are tinged red in winter. The roots are long and fleshy. There are many cultivars available, usually varying in flower color.

 H. micrantha, a western native, adapts easily to home gardens. *H. m.* var. *diversifolia* 'Palace Purple' (hardy in zones 4 to 9) has ivy-shaped leaves and showy foliage—dark bronze red above, beet red below. Long-lasting white flowers bloom in early to midsummer on red stems.

Culture   Coralbells require very little attention. Plant them in well-drained, moist soil. They do best in partial shade and need protection from hot afternoon sun. Set coralbells 1 foot apart in spring in cold areas, anytime elsewhere. Don't plant too deep or crowns may rot. Protect plants with a mulch in cold-winter areas. To propagate, divide clumps or take a leaf cutting with a small portion of the stem attached. Plants need to be divided when they become woody and produce few flowers. Extend the blooming period by removing faded flowers.

Uses   Coralbells make a distinctive ground cover for small areas. They are good edging plants for perennial borders in which roses, delphiniums, peonies, and similar plants grow. They are favored plants of hummingbirds and are attractive as cut flowers.

Hosta
Plantain lily, funkia

Hardy to zone 3 (-40° F)

This large and variable group includes many species and hybrids valued mainly for their dramatic foliage, although some have showy and fragrant flowers as well. They are hardy, long-lived plants, and one of the best for shady areas. All are deciduous—they die to the ground in winter and come back in spring. Hostas provide a feeling of coolness and serenity in summer heat, and great interest from earliest spring to late fall. Plants vary from tiny clumps 8 inches or less in height to bold specimens close to 3 feet tall and 4 feet wide. Leaf color ranges from green, blue (with a chalky cast), and chartreuse, to gold. There is also a wide range of variegation: white or gold edging to central splotches, streaks, and splashes. Some leaves are round, some lance or heart shaped, some cupped (which hold the dew). Leaf textures vary too, albeit subtly; some are ruffled, others dimpled or waffled. Flowering begins in mid-June and is heavy from July until the first frost. The spikes of white, lavender, or lilac blue flowers are fragrant

Hosta undulata 'Albo-marginata' (plantain lily, funkia)

Hypericum calycinum (Aaron's-beard)

and attractive, and may be visited by hummingbirds.

There is some confusion in nomenclature among the hosta hybrids and cultivars. *H. lancifolia* or *H. japonica* (narrow-leaved plantain lily) is one of the low-growing hostas. Leaves are thin, shorter (4 to 6 inches) than the species, and pointed. Flowers are a light blue-purple and appear in late summer. *H. montana* 'Aureo-marginata' has large green leaves with irregular margins of yellow changing to cream during summer. This is a large (more than 42 inches wide) specimen plant that thrives in shade to almost full sun.

H. plantaginea (fragrant plantain lily) has leaves 10 to 18 inches long. Flowers are large, 4 to 5 inches long, on 2-foot stems. These bloom with delicious perfume from late summer into early fall. *H. p.* var. *grandiflora* has light green leaves, 6 inches wide, and is one of the loveliest flowering hostas. It is somewhat tender, however, and, in northern climates, needs protection until established. *H. sieboldiana* has heavily

veined blue-green leaves 10 to 15 inches long, oval to heart shaped and puckered. This species includes 'Frances Williams' (or 'Gold Edge'), which grows in 4-foot-wide clumps of blue-green leaves bordered with a gold edge that deepens in color as summer progresses. Soft, lilaclike flowers bloom in late spring to early summer. 'Elegans' has rounded leaves, 12 inches wide and 15 inches long. White flowers appear in July and August. *H. undulata* has wavy green leaves with white centers. *H. u.* 'Albo-marginata' has oval leaves with broad white margins. Both species and cultivar bloom in late summer. Flowers are lavender purple, with white veins.

Culture Hostas require little maintenance and are quite reliable, although slow to multiply. Plant them in well-drained sandy or loamy soil, high in organic matter. Most do best in medium to dense shade. In northern areas, plant those with blue-green foliage in some sun for good color; plant variegated ones in light

shade. In hotter climates, give ample shade and moisture. Once established, hostas are less sensitive to drought than most other plants. Water carefully. Cold water can spot hot leaves. Renew mulch and fertilize in spring. To propagate, divide plants from early spring to early fall. Hostas transplant with relative ease or can be left in place for decades. Watch for slugs; bait if necessary. Hostas do best in cold-winter areas and are variously hardy. Seedlings are slow to grow and juvenile leaves are often less interesting than mature foliage.

Uses Hostas make excellent border plants and are often used to edge perennial beds and shrubs. Where shade is heavy, these plants are of great practical value. Hostas combine well with astilbe, daylilies, spring bulbs, lily-of-the-valley, ajuga, sedum, wild ginger, lamium, vinca, redtwig and pagoda dogwoods, Korean lilac, azaleas, and viburnums. Or use them singly as accents to break up the monotony of too many smaller-leaved plants.

Hypericum
Aaron's-beard, St. John's wort

Hardy to zone 7 (0° F)

Hypericum calycinum (Aaron's-beard) is a handsome plant that is easy to grow. Foliage is evergreen except in areas with cold winters, where the plant becomes dormant. Leaves are oblong, 2 to 3 inches in length, and bright blue-green. Flowers are about 3 inches across and have bright yellow petals with delicate tufts of orange-yellow stamens rising from the center. They appear through most of the summer, occurring singly and scattered throughout a planting. This sturdy species grows rapidly to a height of 12 to 15 inches and spreads freely by underground shoots.

Culture This plant grows equally well in sun or partial shade and in sandy or loamy soils. It survives drought but looks best when it gets plenty of water. Shear tops each spring to rejuvenate the plant and keep it compact. Propagate by seeds, or more easily by division. Set plants 12 to 18 inches apart.

Iberis sempervirens (evergreen candytuft)

Indigofera kirilowii (Kirilow indigo)

Uses This is a dense ground cover, excellent for mass planting. Its strong root system makes it useful for erosion control. The species can be invasive unless confined. Use a header board or other divider to contain the plants and help keep the planting neat and attractive.

Iberis
Candytuft

Hardy to zone 5 (-20° F)

Iberis sempervirens (evergreen candytuft) is an attractive, 6- to 12-inch-high ground cover that is blanketed with flat white flower clusters in early spring. The clusters, about 2 inches across, appear at the top of stems heavily set with narrow dark green leaves 1½ inches long. The foliage forms a dense mat as the long stems bend to the ground and root again. Several cultivars are more compact. Among them are 'Snowflake', which grows to about 9 inches high, 'Weisser Zwerg', about 6 inches high, and 'Little Cushion', also about 6 inches high.

Culture Candytuft grows best in fertile, well-drained soil and in full sun. It needs regular watering throughout the growing season. Propagate by seeds, cuttings, or division. Cut off old flowers to encourage new growth.

Uses Candytuft is handsome anywhere in the garden. Use it as a small-scale cover, as an edging for walks, in a rock garden, or spilling over a wall.

Ilex
Holly

Hardy to zone 6 (-10° F)

The hollies are highly ornamental trees or shrubs and are among the most widely used of the broadleaf evergreens for low mass plantings. Hollies are noted for their leathery shiny green leaves and clusters of mostly red (sometimes yellow or black) berries. Some plants are self-fertile but most need both a male and a female plant present for the female plant to produce berries. Male plants will not set fruit.

Two types of holly are used extensively in mass ground cover plantings. *Ilex crenata* 'Helleri', grows to 1 foot high and 2 feet wide. *Ilex vomitoria* 'Nana' (dwarf yaupon) is a low, compact shrub with inch-long, narrow, dark green leaves. This very attractive ground cover can be sheared for a more formal look.

Culture Hollies thrive in fertile well-drained garden soil in full sun or light shade. Regular watering is needed throughout the growing season. The plants can be pruned to shape and control growth. Holly leafminer is the most serious insect pest. Spray when damage is first noticed.

Uses Use low-growing hollies in mass plantings for a formal, barrier-creating ground cover. Use 1 or 2 plants together to provide a striking accent anywhere in a landscape that conditions permit. When spaced a foot or less apart, hollies make excellent edgings along walks or adjacent to low stone walls. The berries are a favorite food of many birds.

Indigofera
Indigo

Hardy to zone 5 (-20° F)

Indigofera incarnata (Chinese indigo) is a low (1½ foot), deciduous shrub. A member of the legume family, it develops a strong root system from which tops are renewed each spring. In mild climates the plant remains evergreen. Leaves are divided into many leaflets, each 1 to 3 inches long. Flowers are pink, like small sweet peas, and appear in midsummer. (*I. i.* var. *alba* has white flowers.) This species is hardy to zone 6 (-10° F).

I. kirilowii (Kirilow indigo) is taller (to 3 feet and sometimes as high as 6 feet) and hardier (to -20° F). It does not become as dense as Chinese indigo and is therefore less desirable as a ground cover.

Culture Indigo grows vigorously and requires no extraordinary care. Plant in full sun. Cut back dead tops (with a mower) if they have been winter-killed. In mild climates, prune back to promote better flowering and compact growth. Propagate by seeds, cuttings, or division.

Jasminum nudiflorum (winter yellow jasmine)

Juniperus horizontalis 'Bar Harbor' (creeping juniper)

Uses The strong, interlocking roots of indigo make it a good choice for erosion control on slopes and banks. It is best in large areas. Related species were once used as a source of indigo (deep violet blue) dye.

Jasminum
Jasmine

Hardy to zone 7 (0° F)

These viny shrubs can be deciduous or evergreen and are sometimes invasive. They grow from a central point to form mounds of arching stems that root where they touch the ground. Stems are so green that the plant appears evergreen even after the leaves have fallen. Fragrant yellow flowers, 1 inch across, appear from late February to mid-March. Blooming is sporadic and the plant is seldom heavy with flowers.

Jasminum nudiflorum (winter yellow jasmine) is a deciduous type with 1-inch-wide unscented yellow flowers that appear in midwinter, before the leaves unfold. Branches arch to a height of 3 to 4 feet and spread 4 to 7 feet.

J. officinale (poet's jasmine) is semievergreen with fragrant white flowers that bloom in summer in zones 7 and 8, and in spring, summer, and fall in zones 9 and 10. *J. parkeri* (dwarf jasmine) is a compact, rounded shrub only 12 inches tall with slightly fragrant bright yellow spring flowers. *J. polyanthum* (pink blush jasmine) is covered with clusters of intensely fragrant pale pink flowers in spring through summer. *J. grandiflorum* (Spanish jasmine) has large flowers with a purple tinge. *J. mesnyi* (primrose jasmine), an evergreen, is hardy in zones 8 and 9. Its arching branches are 6 to 10 feet long. Leaves are dark green; flowers are bright lemon yellow and are unscented.

Culture Plant jasmines in sun to partial shade for best growth. They tolerate poor soil and moderate drought but respond well to enriched soil and fertilizer. Jasmines may need some pruning and can be troublesome to remove, especially in warmer regions.

Uses Use these plants for barriers and along stream banks, for massing, or to cover the bare lower branches of taller leggy shrubs.

Juniperus
Juniper

Hardy to zone 3 (-40° F)

Few ground covers have as many desirable qualities as the low-growing junipers. They are evergreen, sturdy, and require little maintenance. *Juniperus chinensis* 'San Jose' (San Jose juniper) is a sturdy, semiprostrate juniper with upward-spreading branches 12 to 18 inches high and 6 feet across. The foliage is compact and sage green. *J. c.* var. *sargentii* 'Glauca' grows into a low mat 8 to 10 feet across and 18 to 24 inches high. Small, scalelike, somewhat feathery foliage is a distinctive blue-green. Native to coastal Japan, this plant often is used along the seashore. *J. c.* var. *sargentii* 'Viridis' has the same form as 'Glauca' but has rich green foliage. These junipers are hardy to -25° F.

J. conferta 'Blue Pacific' has compact, somewhat prickly blue-green foliage. A single plant will grow to 10 feet wide and about 10 inches high. Use this variety in coastal areas and sandy soils. (It can also be grown successfully inland, given enough water.) It tolerates temperatures to -15° F.

J. horizontalis (creeping juniper) is available in many forms. 'Blue Chip' is a low, mounding juniper with scalelike silver blue foliage. It grows about 8 inches high and spreads 8 to 10 feet. 'Bar Harbor' has a distinctive flat-branching growth habit. Feathery gray-green foliage allows some of the main stems to show through. In winter, foliage turns a bronze red color. This variety is very effective planted among large, low rocks. 'Emerson' is a moderately dense, low-branching creeper, 8 to 12 inches high and 6 to 8 feet wide. Scalelike foliage is gray-green. 'Emerald Spreader' has a more delicate appearance than most junipers.

Juniperus communis var. *saxatilis*

Juniperus davurica 'Expansa'

Foliage is feathery, lightly branched, and emerald green. It grows to about 10 inches high, spreading 4 to 6 feet. 'Turquoise Spreader' is similar but has denser foliage with a bluish cast. 'Wiltonii' (blue-rug or Wilton carpet juniper) is among the lowest growing of all the junipers. Its trailing habit and dense, feathery silver blue foliage forms a 4-inch-high mat. A spread of 3 feet after 6 years of growth is typical. These cultivars are hardy to -25° F.

J. h. 'Hughes' is a vigorous, widely spreading juniper with upward-turning branches to 15 inches high. Gray-green leaves have a bluish cast and are somewhat needlelike. 'Douglasii' (Waukegan juniper) has a semierect trailing habit and scalelike bluish green foliage that has a purplish hue in winter. Its mature height is 12 to 16 inches; it spreads 10 feet. 'Plumosa Compacta' has small, feathery bluish green leaves that turn purple in winter; branchlets reach 10 to 12 inches tall. Its spread at maturity is 2 to 4 feet. These three varieties withstand temperatures to -35° F.

J. communis var. *saxatilis* is a prostrate juniper with upward-spreading branchlets; it grows to 1 foot high and 6 feet across. The gray-green foliage is composed of prickly clusters of tiny needlelike leaves. This plant is hardy to -40° F.

J. procumbens 'Nana' (dwarf Japanese garden juniper) is a low-growing, prostrate juniper native to Japan. Foliage is bluish green, dense, and somewhat prickly. The plant has a creeping growth habit and reaches about 2 feet in height. Another cultivar, 'Variegata', has a higher, slightly mounding habit and gray-green foliage with patches of light yellow. Both cultivars are hardy to -25° F.

J. sabina (savin juniper) is available in several good ground cover forms. 'Broadmoor' grows compactly to 1 foot high. Its leaves are tiny, scalelike, green, and prickly. 'Buffalo' is wide spreading, soft, and feathery. Bright green foliage gives this juniper a striking appearance. It grows 10 to 12 inches high and spreads 4 to 6 feet. 'Blue Danube', a native of Austria, has lacy blue-green foliage.

Branches grow upward to about 1 foot and spread 4 feet. 'Scandia' is a rugged juniper with graceful, spreading branches; it grows 1 foot high and up to 3 feet wide. Foliage is dense, lacy and yellow-green. 'Tamariscifolia' (tamarix juniper) has arching branches with dense, lacy blue-green foliage. It has a mounding (to 20 inches), symmetrical growth habit and spreads to 4 feet. This juniper is widely used on slopes, set among rocks, and as a mass planting. *J. sabina* and cultivars are generally hardy to -25 to -30° F.

J. davurica 'Expansa' (or 'Parsonii') is one of the junipers best adapted to the Southeast. It withstands heat and some shade. Branches spread horizontally just above ground level to form a domelike mound 2 to 3 feet high and up to 9 feet across. Foliage is mostly dark green with a tinge of gray. 'Expansa Variegata' has a creamy white foliage variegation; 'Expansa Aureo-spicata' has a butter yellow variegation. This species and its cultivars are generally hardy to -25° F.

J. squamata is a slow-growing dwarf juniper. Foliage is grayish green to bright blue-green with gray-white bands on the upper side. This species may be used in zones 4 to 8 (it is hardy to -30° F), but it does not do as well in the heat and humidity of the Southeast as it does in cooler climates. 'Blue Carpet' has handsome, rich blue-gray-green foliage. It grows 8 to 12 inches tall and spreads to about 4 to 5 feet. 'Blue Star' is low and rounded, about 3 feet high and as wide. The dense foliage is a rich silver blue.

Culture Ground cover junipers grow best in well-drained soil and full sun, and when properly spaced. Amend clay or other heavy soils before planting. Some shade is tolerated, but the plants become woody and lose color. Do not plant junipers too close together. Junipers are slow growers but can spread very wide (up to 10 feet or more in each direction). Resist the tendency to plant more than is necessary. If fast coverage is important, remove plants at a later date to avoid crowding.

Despite their sturdy constitution, junipers may fall

Lamium maculatum 'White Nancy' (spotted deadnettle)

Lantana montevidensis (trailing lantana)

prey to insects and disease. A dry, faded look with patchy brown spots on the top of a plant suggests an infestation of red spider mites. Watch also for evidence of pine needle scale and juniper scale. In the West, the juniper twig girdler is harmful to low-growing junipers. The damage is caused by insect larvae that burrow inside the twigs. Use an oil spray combined with the appropriate insecticide to control these pests. Follow label directions carefully. All junipers, and *J. horizontalis* cultivars in particular, are susceptible to twig blight. This causes twigs and branches to die back. Control with copper sprays in mid- to late summer.

Uses   Although usage varies somewhat by species, the low-growing junipers make excellent small- or large-scale ground covers. They are also very useful in rock gardens.

Lamium
Deadnettle

Hardy to zone 3 (-40° F)

Lamiums are fast-growing deciduous to evergreen perennials that grow to a neat and even cover, rooting as they spread. *L. maculatum* (spotted deadnettle) grows 6 to 12 inches high. Leaves are prominently veined, close growing, and heart shaped to elongated (to 2 inches). They feel furry if rubbed but do not sting like those of their wild relative (hence the "dead" in the common name). Foliage is silver green, turning pink to purple in fall. Flowers are pink, purple, or creamy white and bloom on short spikes anytime from spring to early summer. 'Album' has white flowers; 'Silbergroschen' has silver leaves edged with green and pink flowers; 'White Nancy' has similar leaf markings and white flowers; the leaves of 'Variegatum' have a silver median stripe; 'Shell Pink' has very pale pink flowers; 'Chequers' has pink flowers and marbled leaves; 'Aureum' has leaves splotched with yellow; 'Roseum' has a feather of white on each leaf, and shell pink flowers.

L. galebdolon (formerly *Lamiastrum galeobdolon* and newly reclassified as *Galeobdolon luteum*) is deciduous and less hardy (to zone 4) than *L. maculatum*. Its growth habit is more upright, and it is slightly taller (to 14 inches) at maturity. Flowers are yellow. 'Herman's Pride' has white-flecked leaves and clusters of soft yellow flowers. It is a slower-growing cultivar and less invasive than either species. The leaves of 'Variegatum' are silver with a green midrib and green edges; flowers are yellow. This cultivar spreads rampantly over dry or stony ground.

Culture   Lamiums grow best in shade but tolerate sun if the soil holds sufficient moisture. They do not do well in humid areas (including the southeastern United States) but may come back in fall where they have died back from the heat and humidity of late spring and summer. In areas where they are well adapted, established plants require little attention. Propagate by division, cuttings, or seeds. Trim in late summer and fertilize. Bait for snails.

Uses   Use these colorful plants for highlighting shady corners or for contrast against the solid green leaves of surrounding plants. Plant them to encircle flowering shrubs or as a carpet in a bed of spring tulips, summer callas, or fall-blooming white colchicums.

Lantana
Lantana

Hardy to zone 9 (25° F)

Lantana montevidensis, or sometimes *L. sellowiana* (trailing lantana), is a perennial, evergreen shrub in areas where temperatures do not fall much below freezing. It is characterized by rapid growth and a recurring display of lavender blooms throughout the year. One-inch clusters of tiny flowers appear along the ends of vinelike stems lined with 1-inch-long, oval, dark green leaves. The stems, 3 to 4 feet long, root as they spread, and the plant grows to a height of 1½ to 2 feet. A number of varieties with different flower colors are available.

Leiophyllum buxifolium (sandmyrtle)

Lespedeza thunbergii (bushclover)

Culture Trailing lantana needs sun to thrive. It grows well in poor soil and is drought resistant. Water it only occasionally. Old stands become woody and develop dead patches: Cut these away in early spring. Whiteflies may infest lantana but can be controlled with Orthene®.

Uses Trailing lantana is well suited to large-scale plantings, particularly on steep banks where maintenance is a problem. It is too coarse in texture for covering larger areas in a home landscape but is useful as an accent plant for borders and edging.

Leiophyllum
Sandmyrtle

Hardy to zone 6 (-10° F)

Leiophyllum buxifolium (sandmyrtle) is an attractive evergreen shrub with a rounded habit and tiny, leathery, oval leaves that turn a bronze color in fall. Tiny ¼-inch flowers bloom in 1-inch clusters in late spring. They are pink in the bud, waxy white and frilly, with an extended fringe of stamens, as they open. The species grows to an 18- to 36-inch mound with a 3- to 5-foot spread. There are many cultivars. 'Pinecake' is low and dense. *L. buxifolium prostratum* (Allegheny sandmyrtle) grows only 4 to 10 inches tall.

Culture Sandmyrtles are difficult to start. Set out potted plants in spring in moist but well-drained sandy, acid soil, amended with organic matter. Plant in full sun or partial shade. Water as needed—these plants do not tolerate drought. Sandmyrtle grows slowly and withstands coastal conditions. Prune after bloom. Propagate by cuttings taken in midsummer or by layering.

Uses Sandmyrtle, with its neat habit and slow growth, does well in rock gardens, as an edging, and in seashore gardens.

Lespedeza
Bushclover

Hardy to zone 5 (-20° F)

These deciduous, herbaceous to woody plants include some of the best autumn flowering shrubs. They have trifoliate leaves and bright rose purple or white flowers borne on arching branches through September and October, when few other shrubs are in bloom. The sweet-pea-like flowers cover the upper 2 feet of the branches and often bow them to the ground. Bushclover is drought resistant once established. *Lespedeza thunbergii* (sometimes called *L. sieboldii*) grows 3 to 6 feet in a season and sometimes blooms in June and then again in August-September. It has narrower leaves and is more resistant to deer damage than the species. 'Alba' (white bushclover) grows to 4 to 5 feet with huge clusters of flowers. 'Gibraltar' also grows as high but has blue-green foliage and long racemes of rosy purple flowers.

Culture These plants thrive in full sun. They tolerate poor soil as long as drainage is good. Prune back to 6 to 12 inches before growth starts in spring.

Uses These plants are excellent for erosion control. As members of the legume family, they enrich the soil with nitrogen. They are highly ornamental, with fountains of flowers, and combine well with *Sedum spectabile* 'Autumn Joy' and white *Buddleia*. Bees are attracted to their flowers, quail and other birds to their seeds, deer to their foliage. Young leaves and flowers are edible boiled or fried; mature leaves can be made into tea.

Leucothoe
Leucothoe

Hardy to zone 6 (-10° F)

These low-growing, mostly evergreen shrubs have narrow, pointed leaves that are crimson to bronze when new, glossy green in summer, and red through the winter. Graceful, arching branches are tipped with clusters of urn-shaped flowers of creamy white tinged with pink. *Leucothoe axillaris* (coast leucothoe) grows 2 to 4 feet tall. *L. fontanesiana* (drooping leucothoe) spreads from underground stems and grows

Leucothoe fontanesiana (drooping leucothoe)

Liriope muscari (big blue lilyturf)

3 to 6 feet high. 'Rainbow' is smaller than the species and has leaves variegated with creamy yellow and rosy copper, especially on the new growth. 'Scarletta' grows to only 20 inches tall. New leaves and winter foliage are crimson.

Culture   Leucothoes grow in some sun but do best in partial to full shade. Plant in woodsy, acid soil and keep roots moist. Protect from sun and winter wind. Propagate by seed, cuttings, division, or underground runners. Prune after bloom. Cut oldest branches to the ground every few years to control height and promote vigor. Leucothoes are particularly susceptible to a devastating leaf-spot disease—stressed plants are especially vulnerable. Optimum growing conditions are the best prevention.

Uses   Plant in front of other shrubs such as rhododendrons—any that have scant lower branching. Use with perennials, for a woodland carpet, or cascading over walls. Mass plant to hold banks or slopes.

Liriope
Lilyturf

Hardy to zone 5 (-20° F)

Liriope, one of the most important ground covers in the southern United States, is characterized by clumps of coarse, grasslike mostly dark green leaves up to 24 inches long and ¼ to ¾ inch wide. Like *Ophiopogon* (page 89), with which it is sometimes confused, it is a member of the lily family.

L. muscari, sometimes called *Ophiopogon jaburan* (big blue lilyturf), gets its common name from its 4- to 8-inch-long, spikelike clusters of flowers that are, in fact, more violet than blue. Flowers appear above the leaves from about July into September and are followed by black berries. This species is the tallest of the lilyturfs, growing rather slowly to a height of 2 feet. Among the cultivars are 'Monroe White', with long panicles of white flowers above straplike leaves; 'Lilac Beauty', with lilac purple hyacinth-like flowers and broader leaves; 'Majestic', with lilac panicles

somewhat like those of grape hyacinth but much longer; and 'Silvery Sunproof', with lavender blue flowers and variegated foliage.

L. spicata (creeping lilyturf) is smaller in all aspects, forms a dense cover that spreads by underground stems, has pale lavender flowers, and grows at a moderate rate up to 1 foot high. 'Silver Dragon' has leaves with white stripes.

Culture   These plants have no special soil or light requirements and need only light summer watering. In extremely cold weather leaves turn yellow: Clip them off before new growth starts in spring. Creeping lilyturf is slightly hardier (to -20° F) than big blue lilyturf (hardy to -10° F).

Uses   These plants are excellent as borders along paths, under trees, and in rock gardens, or as fill-in ground cover in large or small areas.

Lonicera
Honeysuckle

Hardy to zone 5 (-20° F)

Of the many species of honeysuckle, most are vines, a few are shrubs, and one, *Lonicera japonica* 'Halliana' (Hall's Japanese honeysuckle), although essentially a vine, is used as a ground cover. It is evergreen in mild climates and semievergreen to deciduous in colder climates. It has the typical twining, climbing (if allowed) honeysuckle growth habit; soft, downy green leaves; and fragrant, trumpet-shaped white flowers that appear in summer and turn a colorful yellow with age. The plant spreads by stems that root as they cover the ground; it is exceptionally fast growing—often invasive. 'Aureoreticulata' is a less vigorous grower and has yellow-veined leaves. 'Purpurea' has purple-tinged leaves and flowers that are purple outside, white inside.

L. nitida (box honeysuckle) grows 3 to 6 feet tall with slender branches and small, thick, glossy leaves up to ½ inch long. Flowers are

Lonicera pileata (privet honeysuckle)

Mahonia aquifolium 'Compacta' (Oregon grape)

Lysimachia nummularia (creeping-charlie)

Mazus reptans (mazus)

long and creamy white, followed by purple berries. 'Baggesen's Gold' has yellow foliage. *L. pileata* (privet honeysuckle) is a spreading shrub that grows into a mound 1 to 3 feet tall and 3 to 5 feet wide. Leaves are oval and 1½ inches long. Fragrant, small white flowers appear in mid-spring and are followed by purple berries. This species is about 10° more cold hardy than box honeysuckle.

Culture   These honeysuckles grow in most soils, in sun or shade, and are drought resistant. They are easily propagated by division or cuttings. Prune them back to prevent woody, scraggly growth.

Uses   Use honeysuckles in informal, medium-to-large areas of the garden where they cannot strangle shrubs or climb trees.

Lysimachia
Creeping-charlie, moneywort

Hardy to zone 3 (-40° F)

Lysimachia nummularia (creeping-charlie) is a rapidly spreading creeper, often considered invasive. Leaves

are small, bright green, and rounded. They are set opposite each other and grow in sufficient number to form a wavy carpet a few inches high. Stems are delicate looking and self-rooting. Bright yellow flowers about ¾ inch in diameter appear through the summer. 'Aurea' has golden foliage and flowers.

Culture   Creeping-charlie grows almost anyplace, in sun or shade, provided that the soil is moist to wet. Propagate by division, starting new plants at any time.

Uses   Creeping-charlie is highly useful in moist, shady places where other plants won't grow. Use around small pools—place near rocks so that the foliage can creep over and around.

Mahonia
Oregon grape, mahonia

Hardy to zone 6 (-10° F)

Mahonia repens (creeping mahonia) retains many of the characteristics of the larger mahonia species and is an especially interesting landscape

subject. It has striking spiny, hollylike bluish green leaves and 1- to 3-inch-long and -wide clusters of bright yellow flowers in spring. After the flowers fall, grapelike dark purple berries form. The plant grows 1 to 2 feet high and spreads rapidly by underground stems. *M. aquifolium* 'Compacta' grows 18 to 24 inches tall and has very glossy leaves that are bronze in winter. Flowers are yellow; small fruits follow. For most ground cover situations, 'Compacta' is superior to the species.

Culture   Although mahonias do fine in full sun, for best appearance plant in filtered shade in well-drained, somewhat moist soil. Propagate by division or from root cuttings. Space the rooted plants about 10 inches apart in spring.

Uses   These are useful plants for medium and small areas, including borders and patio settings with rocks and lattice.

Mazus
Mazus

Hardy to zone 3 (-40° F)

Mazus reptans is a perennial herb that forms a thick, low mat only 1 to 2 inches high. It spreads rapidly, rooting along its stems, and sends up small purplish blue flowers spotted with yellow and white from late spring into summer. It is evergreen in warm-winter areas; elsewhere it freezes to the ground in winter but recovers quickly in spring.

Culture   This alpine plant grows best in a well-drained, moist soil in sun or shade. Propagate by division.

Uses   Mazus is particularly attractive for small-scale planting—in beds, around walks, and as edging. It takes light traffic.

Mentha
Mint

Hardy to zone 7 (0° F)

Mentha requienii (Corsican mint) is the lowest growing of the many species and dozens of cultivars of mint. It spreads rapidly by underground stems,

Mentha requienii (Corsican mint)

Microbiota decussata (Siberian cypress)

Mitchella repens (partridgeberry)

forming a soft green carpet 1 to 3 inches high. Tiny, oval leaves, about ⅛ inch across, grow opposite one another on slender stems and give off a strong minty fragrance when bruised. Tiny lavender flowers appear in midsummer.

Culture This plant grows equally well in sun or light shade. Plant in well-drained, fairly rich soil. Keep the planting area moist. Propagate by division; set new plants 6 inches apart. Corsican mint self-sows. If exposed to freezing temperatures this plant will disappear until spring.

Uses Use Corsican mint in small patches anywhere in the garden. When stepped on it releases a delightfully fresh peppermint scent, so it is especially pleasant planted between stepping-stones.

Microbiota

Siberian cypress, Russian arborvitae

Hardy to zone 3

Microbiota decussata (Siberian cypress) is a low-growing evergreen conifer

that resembles arborvitae in foliage. It forms a dense mat of graceful, arching, fernlike branches, grows only 1 to 2 feet tall, and spreads 6 feet or more. It was first found in Siberia and is very hardy, drought resistant once established, and will grow in shade. Foliage is flat and soft. It turns a somewhat unattractive mauve purple in winter and then back to green in spring. Tiny cones are berrylike.

Culture This is an easy-to-grow and adaptable plant. Good drainage is its only requirement. Propagate by hardwood cuttings or by layering.

Uses Use to cover large areas or under taller, leggy evergreens.

Mitchella

Partridgeberry

Hardy to zone 3 (-40° F)

Mitchella repens (partridge-berry) is a delicate, creeping, perennial plant found in the woods in the eastern United States. Small, round leaves are lustrous and dark green, sometimes variegated with white.

Slender stems grow up to 15 inches long and root where they touch the ground, making flat patches 2 inches tall. In mid-May plants bear pairs of fragrant small, trumpet-shaped white flowers tinged with pink to purple. Showy red berries appear in fall.

Culture Plant in cool, rich, acid soil in the shade. Propagate by seed, division, or cuttings.

Uses This is a useful plant for rock gardens or for the floor of pine groves if the soil is not too dry. Plant with wintergreen, lady's-slipper, trillium, and bunchberry. Quail, grouse, and other birds favor the berries.

Myoporum

Myoporum

Hardy to zone 9 (20° F)

Myoporum parvifolium 'Prostratum' (prostrate myoporum) is a fresh-looking, evergreen shrub, highly rated for coastal California. It grows 3 to 6 inches high and spreads 5 feet or more by means of long, trailing stems. Small white flowers appear in sum-

mer, but it is the foliage and growth form that make the plant such an attractive ground cover. The bright green leaves, ½ to 1 inch long and closely set along the branches, sparkle in the sun. The branches themselves trail gracefully along the ground, rooting where the nodes contact moist soil. This plant is for warm-weather climates. Its growth is quite rapid—up to 3 feet in the first year.

Culture Although prostrate myoporum is grown successfully in many areas of southern and central California, it does best at the seashore, benefiting from the relatively cool temperatures and high humidity during the summer months. The plant has good drought tolerance and is undamaged by ocean spray. Stands become yellow and patchy during the hottest part of the year, even if watered. Well-drained soil is essential. Start plants from tip cuttings or by dividing rooted branches. Set 2 to 3 feet apart for rapid, dense coverage. In confined areas, plantings need to be edged 2 or 3 times a year.

Nandina domestica 'Harbour Dwarf' (heavenly bamboo)

Nepeta mussinii (Persian catnip)

Myoporum parvifolium (myoporum)

Uses Where some summer irrigation can be provided, few plants are better or more attractive than prostrate myoporum for erosion control and fire-hazard reduction on hillside areas along the California coast. The plant is tough but does not take traffic. It is well suited for large-scale landscaping and is neat enough to be used in small, semiformal plantings adjacent to lawns or as cover between flowering trees, on banks, and around patios.

Nandina
Heavenly bamboo

Hardy to zone 6 (0° F)

Nandina domestica (heavenly bamboo) is a well-known landscape shrub favored for years by gardeners on the West Coast and in the southern United States. Like bamboo, it spreads by underground roots and has erect, ringed stems. The broadleaf evergreen foliage is finely cut and changes color with the seasons. Additional year-round interest comes from the upright panicles of small white flowers in spring, which are followed by clusters of green berries that turn brilliant red later in the season. The showy berries remain on the plant throughout the winter.

Cultivars are selected for their disease resistance and color. 'Fire Power' grows 2 feet tall and as wide. Leaves are tinged with red during the summer in some regions (not in the southeastern United States) and become glowing red in winter. 'San Gabriel' (fern-leaved nandina) has airy, fernlike foliage. New growth is apricot-colored, gradually becoming bright green before turning brilliant crimson in winter. 'Harbour Dwarf', reaching only 12 to 18 inches tall, is dense and graceful. It is semievergreen where winters reach 0° F, orange to bronzy red in fall, a soft green-tinted pink in spring. 'Woods Dwarf' has attractive red winter color and grows to 3 feet tall. 'Purpurea' has glossy green foliage tinged with purple in spring and summer and brilliant scarlet in cold weather. It grows only 18 to 24 inches tall with a stiff, upright form. 'Moonbay' and 'Gulfstream' are also very attractive and useful, low-growing, massing forms.

Culture These plants are easy to grow, drought tolerant, and have few problems. They tolerate shade, but foliage colors more dramatically when the plants are grown in full sun. Rich, well-drained soil is best. Prune the canes back at staggered heights to encourage foliage to develop over the entire plant and to prevent legginess. A little cold brings out the best in nandinas—they can be disappointing in very warm climates.

Uses Plant in groups, as a screen, an accent, or in foundation plantings. These make fine container plants, which can stretch their range.

Nepeta
Catnip

Hardy to zone 5 (-20° F)

Nepeta mussinii (Persian catnip) has small, sturdy gray-green leaves that make this herb an attractive ground cover. Lavender flower spikes on stems 1 to 2 feet high are produced in large quantities in early summer.

Culture Persian catnip requires light, well-drained soil, full sun, and periodic watering in summer. Remove dead flower spikes after spring bloom to encourage a second flowering in fall.

Uses This plant is most attractive in large patches in a rock garden, as a border, or behind a low-growing cover.

Ophiopogon
Mondograss

Hardy to zone 7 (0° F)

Dense clumps of long, ⅛-inch-wide leaves that arch over into mounds 8 to 10 inches high characterize *Ophiopogon japonicus* (mondograss). Leaves are dark green and coarsely textured. Small pale purple flowers, mostly hidden among the leaves, appear in July and August, followed by pea-sized blue fruit. Mondograss spreads by means of fleshy, subsurface stems. The growth rate is quite slow

Ophiopogon japonicus (mondograss)

Pachysandra procumbens (Allegheny spurge)

until the plant is well established. 'Nana', a dwarf cultivar, grows about half as high as the species.

O. jaburan is similar in size and growth habit to *Liriope muscari* (page 86); each plant is often mistaken for the other. *O. jaburan* has green rather than brownish stems, and white, more drooping, less tightly clustered flowers. *O. jaburan* 'Variegatus' is a low-growing cultivar with striated white leaves.

Culture　These plants are adaptable to most well-drained soils. In coastal areas they grow in full sun; plant in partial shade elsewhere. In all areas, regular summer watering is required. Mondograss needs more frequent watering if exposed to full sun in a mass planting. New plants can be started by dividing clumps; set *O. japonicus* plants 6 inches *apart, O. jaburan* 12 inches apart.

Uses　Plant mondograss in masses in the shade of a mature tree. In a shaded patio setting, place a few dozen plants about 8 inches apart with

baby's tears (*Soleirolia soleirolii,* page 100) in between. Mondograss also makes a handsome border along paths and is useful in defining and separating a lawn and a flower bed. *O. jaburan* is most effective where its attractive flowers (good for cutting) and violet blue fruits can be seen up close, as in entryways, near fences or buildings, and under large trees.

Pachysandra
Spurge

Hardy to zone 4 (-30° F)

Pachysandra terminalis (Japanese spurge) is an evergreen perennial widely used as a ground cover for shady locations. Leaves are 1½ to 4 inches long, veined, dark green, spoon shaped, and lightly toothed near the ends. They grow in whorls at the top of stems that creep along as underground runners and then grow upright to a height of 6 to 8 inches. Spikes of tiny, fluffy greenish white flowers appear in late winter to early spring and are interesting but not conspicuous. Small white

berries may follow. This species is an elegant and ideal ground cover for shady gardens in cool regions. 'Emerald' or 'Green Carpet', hardier than the species and more tolerant of adverse conditions, is a bit shorter and denser with better winter color. 'Variegata' (silver edge spurge) has lighter green leaves with a narrow margin of creamy white. It is slightly less vigorous than the species. 'Green Sheen' has dark green leaves with a lustrous, almost mirrorlike surface.

P. procumbens (Allegheny spurge) is native to the Appalachian Mountains, evergreen in zone 8, deciduous in zones 5 to 7. It resists *Volutella pachysandrae,* a fungal disease known to kill entire plantings of Japanese spurge. The leaves of Allegheny spurge are not as lustrous as those of Japanese spurge but are attractively mottled with gray to blue-green. Fragrant, 2- to 4-inch spires of pinkish white to purple flowers appear in early spring and are especially attractive.

Culture　Spurge is a slow spreader. Plant it in a neutral-to-acid soil, rich in humus, with fairly constant moisture. Protect it from winter wind and sun: It turns yellow and may die out when exposed. Foot traffic crushes the succulent stems, so use stepping-stones or paths through it. These plants do not tolerate poor drainage or adverse conditions, but they withstand some drought once established. Increase by cuttings in summer or by root divisions set out in fall or spring. Plant 6 to 12 inches apart. Water well the first season. Fertilize twice each year. In hot locations with poor air movement, watch for scale, red spider mite, and fungal disease. To control, use sprays recommended by qualified nursery personnel.

Uses　These plants are outstanding ground covers for mass planting under trees (where they compete well with tree roots), as an edging around shrubs, on slopes, or in small areas too shady for grass. Spurges do not do well in coastal areas or in the humidity of the Deep South.

Parthenocissus quinquefolia (Virginia creeper, woodbine)

Paxistima canbyi (canby pachistima)

Pernettya mucronata (pernettya)

Parthenocissus

Virginia creeper, woodbine

Hardy to zone 3 (-35° F)

Parthenocissus quinquefolia (Virginia creeper) is a rambling, deciduous vine native to eastern North America. It is commonly found in woodlands and is especially visible in fall, when it turns bright red. Leaves are divided into leaflets that are each attached at the same point and are 2 to 6 inches long, depending on the variety. Leaflets are heavily veined and have toothed edges. Inconspicuous flowers are followed by attractive blue fruits that are eaten by birds. *P. tricuspidata* (Boston ivy) is a close relative and has 3-lobed, maplelike leaves.

Culture Virginia creeper is fast and easy to grow. Spaced widely, it covers a large area remarkably fast, although not very densely. Spaced closely (3 to 5 feet apart) in rich, moist soil, the plants can make a solid cover in one season. Virginia creeper takes heavy shade. It propagates easily by layers that form naturally; it can also be grown from seeds sown in spring. It is vulnerable to Japanese beetle infestation but controls are available. Check with a local nursery.

Uses Virginia creeper readily climbs trellises and drapes over walls, attaching itself to objects by means of adhesive discs. Do not plant where it can climb (and maybe smother) shrubs or trees. It is best used to cover large, barren, rocky areas where little else grows; it also makes an excellent slope cover. It is well suited to naturalistic areas, where its growth doesn't need to be controlled. Because of its salt tolerance, Virginia creeper can often be found in eastern coastal gardens.

Paxistima

Pachistima

Hardy to zone 5 (-10° F)

Paxistima canbyi (canby pachistima) is a 1-foot-high, low-maintenance ground cover. It has been known but little used for many years and is native to the mountains of Virginia and the Carolinas. Similar to boxwood, it has narrow, ¼-inch-wide and ¼- to 1-inch-long, evergreen leaves that color slightly in areas with cold winters. The plant is long-lived and becomes denser over time. *P. myrsinites* (Oregon boxwood) is native to the West Coast. Its leaves are slightly larger, and it can become twice as tall as *P. canbyi;* prune to keep it low.

Culture Canby pachistima grows well in either full sun or partial shade, although it usually becomes denser in full sun. It is native to rocky soil, but any well-drained, slightly acidic garden soil is satisfactory. Branches root as they spread. Propagate by division or cuttings. Oregon boxwood is well suited to coastal locations; it does best in cool, moist areas in full sun. It can also be grown inland with some shade and lots of water.

Uses Use canby pachistima under trees and as a low hedge. It is also a good choice for naturalistic and rock gardens.

Pernettya

Pernettya

Hardy to zone 6 (-5° F)

Pernettya mucronata is a handsome, dwarf evergreen shrub much admired for its ½-inch-wide white to dark purple berries that appear in great numbers from autumn through winter. The berries are preceded by a fine display of tiny, urn-shaped white flowers. Berries and flowers are set off by small, shiny dark green leaves that turn bronze in winter. The shrub spreads by underground runners, forming wide clumps up to 1½ feet.

Culture Except in hot areas, pernettya is best grown in full sun; in shade it tends to become rank and invasive. It does not grow in the East, or along the southeastern coast of the United States. It needs acid soil and generally cool, moist conditions. It is a good idea to group several of the color varieties together to ensure cross-pollination and an ample production of fruit. Propagate by division or cuttings.

Uses This plant is effective as a border near an entryway

Perovskia atriplicifolia (Russian sage)

Phalaris arundinacea var. *picta* (ribbongrass)

Phlox subulata (moss pink or moss phlox)

or along a path. It is also attractive as a low hedge adjoining a garden pool.

Perovskia
Russian sage

Hardy to zone 4 (-30° F)

Perovskia atriplicifolia (Russian sage) is a graceful, feathery subshrub with finely cut silver gray foliage. It grows in mounded clumps, 3 to 5 feet tall. Blue flower spikes, 9 to 12 inches long, appear from July to September. Buds and stems have a whitish down. Foliage is fragrant when crushed. 'Blue Spire' grows to 3 feet and has deeply lobed leaves and abundant flowers.

Culture *P. atriplicifolia,* like most sages, does best in full sun and a slightly acid soil. Prune branches back to live wood in spring if they die back in winter. Propagate with stem cuttings taken in early spring.

Uses This plant should be used more. It is striking in mass plantings, with ornamental grasses such as blue oatgrass, or as a specimen. Use it also as a cut flower plant.

Phalaris
Ribbongrass

Hardy to zone 3 (-40° F)

Phalaris arundinacea var. *picta* (ribbongrass) has long been used decoratively. It is very hardy and is tolerant of poor growing conditions. Its height is typically 2 feet, and its leaves are 6 to 12 inches long with white stripes. Foliage is striking from spring to midsummer. It browns in fall but remains erect. Ribbongrass spreads by underground runners and is very invasive.

Culture Ribbongrass is most vigorous in rich, well-drained soil, although leaf variegation may disappear in these conditions. In heavy or wet soil, growth slows and the plant is more manageable. It turns brown where water applications are insufficient. In the garden, contain ribbongrass in sections of concrete or clay drainpipe. Once established, it is difficult to eradicate.

Uses Ribbongrass is very handsome in a perennial border or as a backdrop for lower-growing, flowering plants.

Phlox
Phlox

Hardy to zone 3 (-40° F)

Phlox subulata (moss pink or moss phlox) is a mat-forming perennial that produces a 4- to 6-inch-high carpet. The brilliantly colored, ½-inch flowers, ranging in color from white to various shades of pink and red, cover the needlelike foliage completely from late spring into midsummer. Individual plants grow in clumps, spreading rapidly by means of trailing stems. Different-colored cultivars are available, including 'White Delight', 'Red Wings', and 'Emerald Cushion Blue'.

Culture Moss pink is hardy and sturdy and grows in most soils with good drainage. Plant in full sun. Because seeds are not reliable in reproducing to type, propagate by division. In spring, set out new plants 12 to 18 inches apart. To stimulate growth and keep plants compact, mow them about halfway to the ground after they flower.

Uses Moss pink makes an attractive, small-scale border or accent plant. It can also be used dramatically and to great advantage in large-scale plantings.

Phyla
Lippia

Hardy to zone 8 (20° F)

Phyla nodiflora (also known as *Lippia canescens*) is a perennial, evergreen herb. With some exceptions, it makes an excellent lawn alternative in warm climates, forming a dense, flat mat 1 to 2 inches high. Its green foliage spreads rapidly by surface runners. Tiny lavender flowers spotted with yellow appear from spring through summer. They attract bees, a potential liability when the plant is used as a lawn substitute.

Culture Lippia grows well in most soils in sun or partial shade, but better in sun. It withstands extreme heat and is very drought resistant. Propagate by division, planting small pieces of sod 4 inches apart for fast cover.

Uses Mow off the plant's flowers to create a tough, flat green mat that is very suitable

Phyla nodiflora (lippia)

Polygonum cuspidatum var. *compactum* (Japanese knotweed)

Polystichum polyblepharum (tassel fern)

for use as a lawn substitute in an informal setting. Lippia is also effective around small garden pools, where it can creep among rocks and up small slopes.

Pittosporum
Mock orange

Hardy to zone 9 (20° F)

Pittosporum tobira (mock orange) is an evergreen shrub or small tree 6 to 15 feet or more high. 'Wheeler's Dwarf' grows to about 2 feet and is useful as a ground cover. It has a mounding growth habit and grows at a moderate rate. Typically, mock orange has thick, leathery leaves, roughly oval in shape and ¾ to 1½ inches long. Leaves are dark green and densely set along the branches, most heavily at the tips. Orange-scented white flowers that become cream-colored with age appear in dense clusters at the branch tips in spring. A variegated cultivar is available that grows somewhat higher and is distinguished by light green leaves etched in creamy white at the tips.

Culture This sturdy plant grows well in most soils in full sun or partial shade. Although fairly drought resistant, it does best with regular watering throughout the year. Keep pruning to a minimum. Propagate by cuttings.

Uses These are popular landscape plants in mild-climate areas, where they are effective as a foreground for taller plants. They also make excellent borders, particularly along stepping-stone paths.

Polygonum
Knotweed, pink clover blossom

Hardy to zone 5 (-20° F)

The few species of *Polygonum* (most newly reclassified *Persicaria;* some *Fallopia*) that qualify as ornamental ground covers are mostly mat-forming, creeping perennials that spread rapidly and invasively. Nonetheless, they can be useful and do have attractive foliage and a long blooming period. *P. capitata* grows in mounds 5 to 8 inches high with wiry, trailing reddish stems loosely covered by inch-long, elliptical dark green

to pinkish leaves and small pink flower heads that bloom most of the year. 'Magic Carpet' is one of the best cultivars of this species.

P. vacciniifolia is a taller (to 9 inches), vigorous, less weedy looking plant than *P. capitata*, mainly because of its upright, 3- to 4-inch-long rosy flower spikes. *P. cuspidatum* var. *compactum* (reclassified *Fallopia japonica* var. *compacta* and commonly called Japanese knotweed) is the hardiest of this group, easily surviving harsh winters in exposed locations. It grows 15 to 18 inches tall and blooms with pink flowers from mid-summer to frost. Because it is fast growing and tolerant of poor soil, it can be extremely invasive. Use it only where it has plenty of room to spread or where its toughness is needed. *P. affinis* (Himalayan fleeceflower) has basal leaves 3 to 4 inches long. Small bright rose flowers closely bunched on a 3-inch spike at the end of a 6-inch red stalk bloom in mid- to late summer.

Culture These plants grow best in full sun in any soil that

has good drainage. Water them occasionally in areas where summers are dry. Propagate by division or cuttings. *P. capitata* is tender to frost but comes back if the freeze is not too severe. *P. vacciniifolia* is hardy to 5° F, *P. cuspidatum* var. *compactum* to -20° F.

Uses Use these plants in informal settings and where they can be contained. *P. capitata* has been used effectively in southern California as a parking strip planting. *P. vacciniifolia* makes a good cover on moderate slopes and can be quite striking in a rock garden. The neat habit of *P. affinis* makes it useful for edging a border, pool, or slow-moving stream.

Polystichum
Shield fern

Hardy to zone 3 (-40° F)

Polystichum comprises a large group of ferns, including many natives of North American forests. They are hardy and usually evergreen, with sword-shaped fronds. These plants are similar to *Dryopteris*

Potentilla fruticosa 'Princess' (shrubby cinquefoil)

Pyracantha koidzumii (Santa Cruz pyracantha)

(page 70), but the rough, saw-toothed edges of shield fern fronds are a typical, distinguishing characteristic. *P. acrostichoides* (Christmas fern) is native from Nova Scotia to Florida. The common name derives from the commercial availability of its fronds for Christmas decorations. *P. munitum* (western sword fern) is native to an area extending from Alaska south to California and east to Montana. Its fronds are leathery, 2 to 3½ feet long, and sometimes 10 inches wide at the base.

Culture   Plant shield ferns in moist areas, full shade, and a humus-rich soil. Propagate by dividing the underground runners in spring.

Uses   Use these plants in shady woodland areas.

Potentilla
Cinquefoil

Hardy to zone 3 (-40° F)

The cinquefoils are evergreen and deciduous perennials and shrubs that make highly serviceable, ornamental ground covers. They have 5 wedge-shaped, coarsely toothed bright green leaflets; small, roselike flowers; and a rapid growth rate, spreading by surface runners.

Potentilla crantzii (spring cinquefoil) is the lowest-growing species, forming a dense, matlike cover 3 to 6 inches high. Bright yellow flowers, about ⅜ inch across, appear singly but in great numbers from spring well into summer. *P. nepalensis* 'Miss Willmott' grows to 10 inches high, has correspondingly larger leaflets, and flowers that are a striking deep red. *P. cinerea* (alpine cinquefoil), popular in the Pacific Northwest, has pale yellow flowers and grows in tufts up to 4 inches high.

P. fruticosa (shrubby cinquefoil) is a low, deciduous shrub with bright yellow blooms (like large buttercups) from June through frost. 'Abbotswood' grows to 2 feet tall with pure white flowers and bluish green foliage. 'Coronation Triumph' grows to 4 feet in height and does well in the Midwest. 'Goldfinger' is a delicate, graceful shrub that grows slowly to 4 feet high and 2 to 4 feet wide. It has feathery foliage and 2-inch-wide yellow flowers. 'Jackman's Variety' reaches 3 to 4 feet in height and has bright golden yellow blooms and dark green foliage. 'Primrose Beauty' grows 2 to 3 feet tall and has pale yellow flowers with dark centers and grayish green foliage. Dozens of other cultivars are available.

Culture   These plants grow in full sun in all but desert areas and also do well in shade. Plant in well-drained soil and water regularly. Prune *P. fruticosa* occasionally. Propagate *P. fruticosa* by cuttings, others by division. *P. cinerea* and *P. n.* 'Miss Willmott' are the hardiest (to -40° F). *P. crantzii* is less hardy (to -10° F). *P. fruticosa* does not perform well in the warmer winter areas—zones 7 to 10.

Uses   Cinquefoils are excellent for medium-scale plantings on slopes, under high-branched trees, or among groups of rocks.

Pyracantha
Firethorn, pyracantha

Hardy to zone 6 (-10° F)

The genera *Pyracantha* and *Cotoneaster* (page 66) are composed of botanically similar evergreen shrubs that are sometimes difficult to distinguish at first glance. The easiest identifiable difference is that most pyracanthas have thorns, whereas cotoneasters do not. *P. koidzumii* 'Santa Cruz' (Santa Cruz pyracantha) has glossy, oval dark green leaves 1½ to 2½ inches long and serrated at the tips. Masses of short-lived, tiny white flowers appear in spring. In fall, clusters of berrylike bright red fruits, attractively framed against the leaves, appear along the branch ends. The fruits remain on the branches for several months. The plant has a prostrate, rapidly spreading growth habit and mounds to 2 to 4 feet in height. 'Ruby Mound' is notable for its long, graceful, intertwining branches. In 5 years a single plant mounds to 2½ feet and spreads to 10 feet.

Rhaphiolepis umbellata (Indian-hawthorn)

Rhus aromatica (fragrant sumac)

Culture These plants grow in most soils, doing best in sunny locations. Although regular watering is needed, keep the soil on the dry side to stimulate fruit production. Prune upward-growing branches occasionally. Fire-thorns are subject to attacks of fire blight, a bacterial disease that causes the foliage and stems to turn black, as if burned. Trim out dead and diseased branches to control. Lace bugs and aphids may also be a problem; control with Orthene®. Propagate fire-thorns from cuttings rooted in a light potting mix. In spring, set out rooted plants about 18 inches apart.

Uses These decorative plants are excellent as borders, rough hedges, or trailing down rocky slopes. The ripe fruits are edible and can be used to make a bland jelly.

Rhaphiolepis
Indian-hawthorn

Hardy to zone 8 (10° F)

This is a spreading, dense, evergreen shrub grown mostly in the southern United States. Leaves are alternate, glossy, and leathery. They grow from 1½ to 2½ inches long and 1 inch wide with a few teeth on the margin near the tip. Young leaves are bronze, slightly woolly, and tufted at the ends of young branches. Stems are fairly stiff, green when young, then covered with fine red hairs, and finally gray-green to a smooth gray-brown when mature. Showy clusters of pink or white flowers bloom from midwinter until late spring, with a possible second bloom in fall. Bright blue-black berries in the same clusters follow the flowers in mid- to late summer.

The species *Rhaphiolepis indica* is rarely grown but many varieties are available. *R. umbellata* is wide spreading and has broad, roundish leaves. Flowers are white. Cultivars can be from either species. *R. i.* 'Fascination' forms a small, compact mound with dense branching and dark green foliage. Flowers are rose-colored with a white center. 'Springtime' has bronzy green foliage and pink blooms. It is a more vigorous grower and less compact. 'Enchantress' is smaller and more compact than the species and has rose pink flowers in large clusters. 'Snow White' has light green foliage and pure white flowers in early spring to summer and is disease resistant.

Culture Where it is adapted, Indian-hawthorn tolerates dry conditions but does best with regular watering and fertilizing. Plant it in full sun for best bloom and in fertile, well-drained soil. Prune after it flowers to keep plants compact and encourage later bloom. A leaf-spot disease can cause foliage drop in certain cultivars, particularly in moist, shady areas. Check with qualified nursery personnel for appropriate controls.

Uses Indian-hawthorn makes an attractive, large-scale ground cover. Use it also for foundation plantings, as a low divider, or, with regular pruning, as an informal hedge.

Rhus
Sumac

Hardy to zone 3 (-40° F)

Rhus aromatica (fragrant sumac) grows 3 to 4 feet high (sometimes as high as 10 feet) and spreads 6 to 8 feet. It has large, aromatic, compound leaves with 3 leaflets. Flowers are small, yellow, borne on short spikes, and bloom in spring before the leaves unfold. Fruit is in velvety dark red clusters that stand above the leaves. Foliage turns brilliant orange and then scarlet in fall. Fragrant sumac grows quickly and is often seen covering banks along roadsides. 'Green Mound' grows to 4 feet as a rounded, dense shrub. 'Low Grow' reaches only 2 feet in height and has small, fragrant flowers.

Culture Sumac does well in poor, dry soil that is well drained. Plant in sun or partial shade. Water it occasionally.

Uses Its fast-spreading roots and dense foliage make this a good bank cover to control erosion. It is most effective in mass plantings.

Ribes alpinum (alpine currant)

Rosa rugosa 'Frau Dagmar Hastrup' (rose)

Ribes

Currant, gooseberry

Hardy to zone 3 (-40° F)

This genus includes some suitable ground covers, including deciduous, somewhat prickly shrubs 3 or more feet tall that spread by underground runners. Small green to violet flowers in fairly large clusters appear in spring. Berries are lime green to maroon red, strung in clusters along the stem, and usually ripen in early July. Leaves are alternate, lobed, and light to medium green.

Ribes alpinum (alpine currant) produces smooth scarlet currants when properly pollinated. (The 2 sexes are on different plants.) 'Green Mound' grows 2 to 3 feet tall and equally wide. Flowers are greenish yellow, and fruit is scarlet. Bright green foliage turns golden yellow in fall. 'Nana', 'Pumilum', and 'Compacta' are compact, low-growing cultivars.

Culture   *Ribes* species should have as much sun as possible. They will, however, take more shade than most fruiting plants; some will do well on the north side of buildings. They do best in good garden loam but tolerate poorer soils. Plant in fall to ensure early spring flowering. Thin canes yearly leaving 8 to 10 per plant—for best fruit. *Ribes* are alternate hosts for white pine blister rust. Do not plant them near white pines.

Uses   Use these in foundation plantings or under trees with high crowns. Combine them with plum trees in a mixed border or let them cascade over a wall or slope. Plant the thorny ones to discourage foot traffic or under windows for security. These plants also grow well in containers.

Rosa

Rose

Hardy to zone 4 (-25° F)

Many roses make fine ground covers with their variously fragrant blooms, attractive edible fruit, and colorful fall foliage. But choose plant types carefully: Some require pruning, spraying, and fertilizing, as would a regular rose garden. *Rosa banksiae* 'Lutea' (Lady Bank's rose), a climbing evergreen, is aphid resistant, almost thornless, and thrives in zones 7 and 8. 'Alba Plena' has fragrant double white flowers; 'Lutescens' has single yellow ones. *R. rugosa* is a vigorous, very hardy, deciduous shrub with prickly stems. It grows to 3 to 8 feet tall. Leaves are bright green and crinkly; flowers are 3 to 4 inches across and very fragrant. 'Frau Dagmar Hastrup', one of the best disease-resistant cultivars, has fragrant light-pink flowers, showy hips, and excellent fall color. *R. wichuraiana* (memorial rose) and its many cultivars are relatively problem-free prostrate plants that bloom only once in late spring. Trailing stems root as they spread, growing 10 to 12 feet in length in one season.

Some of the newer shrub roses include 'Bonica', with medium pink double flowers. In cold-winter areas this variety may die back to the ground but will resprout and bloom again by June. 'Pink-', 'White', and 'Red Meidiland' have clusters of single flowers all season and reddish fruits for winter interest. These make good mass or barrier plantings. 'Carefree Beauty' has an open habit and fragrant medium pink flowers from June until first frost.

For the far north, choose such hardy and disease-free varieties as 'Champlain', with fragrant dark red flowers; 'Charles Albanel', with medium red blooms, also fragrant, and a long blooming period; 'John Davis', with perfumy pink blooms; or 'Rugosa Ottawa', whose purple flowers are sparse but bloom over a long season.

Culture   Roses grow best in well-prepared soil and full sun but tolerate poor soil. They layer naturally: Dig the layers to propagate, or take cuttings. Plant 4 to 5 feet apart. Tie canes of climbers to short stakes at the tips to force flowering along the length of the cane. Pull out weeds when they appear—a rose cover is not dense enough to prevent

Rosmarinus officinalis 'Lockwood de Forest' (dwarf rosemary)

Sagina subulata (Irish moss)

Santolina virens (lavender-cotton)

their encroachment. Prune out old canes or cut to the ground occasionally to rejuvenate the plants. Climbing roses do well in the right situations, but they can be rampant and difficult to remove.

Uses Roses are unsurpassed for rapidly covering large, poor soil areas and sandy shorelines. Use them in difficult situations, such as seaside plantings, in sandy soil, or along banks or slopes.

Rosmarinus
Rosemary

Hardy to zone 8 (10° F)

This woody evergreen is well known in its taller form for its various herbal uses. *Rosmarinus officinalis* 'Prostratus' (dwarf rosemary) grows slowly, creeping along the ground and spreading 4 to 8 feet. Its normal height is about 8 inches, but a mass planting can be expected to mound up to 2 feet, particularly as plants mature. Like other members of the *Rosmarinus* genus, 'Prostratus' has aromatic, narrow

deep green leaves and tiny clusters of ½-inch-long light blue flowers. These plants bloom throughout most of the year but most heavily in winter and spring. A cultivar of *R. officinalis* widely used in southern California is 'Lockwood de Forest'. It is similar to 'Prostratus' but has some erect branches that grow to 2 feet and foliage that is a little lighter in color.

Culture Dwarf rosemary grows well in almost any soil as long as it has good drainage: It does not tolerate soggy soil. The plant is drought resistant, but water it occasionally in very dry areas. Propagate by seed or cuttings, setting new plants 2 feet apart. Control and rejuvenate woody, older plants by cutting out dead wood.

Uses Dwarf rosemary is excellent as a border or low hedge, cascading over a low wall, or grown on a slope to prevent erosion.

Sagina
Irish moss, scotch moss

Hardy to zone 5 (-20° F)

Sagina subulata (Irish moss) and *S. subulata* 'Aurea' (Scotch moss) are evergreen, perennial herbs, varying only in color: Irish moss is deep green; Scotch moss is yellow-green. They grow in dense, rounded tufts of tiny, awl-shaped leaves. Tufts grow together by means of creeping stems, rapidly forming a soft, mossy carpet 3 to 4 inches high. Tiny white flowers appear in summer.

Culture These plants grow equally well in full sun or light shade. To thrive, they need rich, well-drained soil and enough water to keep them moist but not soggy. Propagate by division.

Uses The growth habit and interesting texture of Irish and Scotch moss make them ideal for use between stepping-stones and other places where they can fill in the gaps between rocks or paving blocks. They take some foot traffic.

Santolina
Lavender-cotton

Hardy to zone 7 (0° F)

Santolina chamaecyparissus (lavender-cotton) is an evergreen shrub grown chiefly for its distinctive aromatic light gray foliage. Leaves are finely cut, woolly, and green tinged. They densely cover the top 6 to 8 inches of woody stems that can rise as high as 2½ feet. For a month or so in summer, the foliage is partially covered by a profusion of small, round bright yellow flower heads. This is a sturdy species that spreads rapidly by creeping stems. A dwarf form, 'Nana', is available in some nurseries. *S. virens* is similar to *S. chamaecyparissus* but has more delicate deep green foliage and pale yellow flowers. It grows about half as high and is clumpier in form.

Culture Lavender-cotton grows in any well-drained (including sandy or gravelly) soil in full sun. It is exceptionally drought and salt resistant and requires only occasional watering in summer. It dies to the ground in very cold areas but usually

Sarcococca hookerana var. *humilis* (small Himalayan sarcococca)

Sedum spurium 'Dragon's Blood' (stonecrop)

recovers. To keep foliage compact and to prevent woody stems from showing, prune the plant once a year to 1 foot or less in height. Propagate from cuttings taken in spring or fall.

Uses Left untouched, lavender-cotton can serve as an informal planting against a wood fence. Clip it to create a semiformal, low hedge. Use it as an accent plant on a patio or other small area. Sachets made from the dried foliage (very powdery—use tightly woven material) have long been used as a moth repellent.

Sarcococca
Sarcococca

Hardy to zone 5 (-20° F)

Sarcococca hookerana var. *humilis* (small Himalayan sarcococca) is an attractive, broadleaf evergreen shrub noteworthy for its adaptability to dense shade. It stays low, rarely exceeding 2 feet, and spreads several feet by underground runners. Foliage is glossy and dark green. Leaves are 1 to 2 inches long and about ½ inch wide. Fragrant white flowers bloom in late

winter and last into spring. These are followed by black berries.

Culture Plant sarcococca in the shade, in acidic soil generously amended with organic matter. Direct sunlight or reflected heat are damaging, as is too much wind. Water frequently until the plant becomes established, then water regularly to prevent it from drying out. Pinch stem tips to promote horizontal spreading and dense growth. Propagate by cuttings, seed, or division of the creeping roots. Check for scale insects—control infestations with Orthene®, malathion, or carbaryl.

Uses This plant is excellent as a mass planting in heavily shaded areas where little else grows, or as a low border in front of such tall-growing shrubs as rhododendrons and camellias.

Sedum
Stonecrop

Hardy to zone 3 (-35° F)

There are more than 300 species and at least twice as many varieties of *Sedum*.

There are tiny ones that form mats only 1 to 2 inches high and others that reach 2 feet. A few flower abundantly; others have inconspicuous blooms. The beauty of the plants is in the shape and color of their leaves. *S. acre* (mossy or goldmoss stonecrop) has tiny leaves less than ¼ inch long. It is a vigorous grower that reaches a height of only 2 inches and stays green through the winter (to -35° F).

S. album is a fast-growing, creeping evergreen that forms a green mat 3 to 6 inches high. In summer it sends up 8-inch stems covered at the top by delicate, branching clusters of tiny, star-shaped white flowers that attract bees. There are a number of varieties, some with purple foliage and yellow-green or pinkish flowers. This species is hardy to -20° F. *S. anglicum* is a popular, hardy, evergreen creeper that forms a dense, mosslike dark green mat about 3 inches high. Pinkish white flowers cover 3- to 5-inch stems in summer. *S. anglicum* is hardy to -20° F.

S. brevifolium, an evergreen creeper, forms a bright green mat 2 inches high. It has wiry, somewhat woody stems and, in summer, white flowers streaked with pink. It makes a good rock garden plant and is hardy to -20° F. *S. confusum* is a relatively tender sedum (hardy to 10° F). It is an evergreen, somewhat shrubby, branching plant, about 1 foot high, that fills in quickly. The leaves are light green; the summer flowers are yellow. *S. dasyphyllum* is a handsome evergreen (annual in very cold climates) that forms a low-tufted (1 to 2 inches) bluish green mat lightly covered by white flowers in summer and fall. It needs full sun and is hardy to 0° F.

S. rubrotinctum, commonly known as pork and beans or whisky nose, is another popular variety. Stems are 3 to 6 inches long; top halves are covered with clusters of beanlike green leaves that become bronzy red with exposure to full sun. This plant self-seeds readily, so it can crowd out smaller species. It produces yellow flowers in spring, but it is the evergreen

Sempervivum tectorum (hen and chickens)

Skimmia japonica (skimmia)

foliage that makes it a desirable ground cover. It is hardy to 10° F. *S. oaxacanum* is a spreading, evergreen plant with 6-inch-long brownish stems covered mostly at the ends with rosettes of thick grayish green leaves. Yellow flowers appear in spring. This plant is hardy to 10° F.

S. palmeri (compressum), an attractive, flowering evergreen, has fleshy gray-green leaves in loose rosettes at the top of stems 6 to 8 inches high. Beautiful yellow flowers are produced from April to summer. Compressum is hardy to 10° F. *S. sarmentosum* is a hardy (to -40° F), spreading evergreen with yellow-green leaves. It grows about 6 inches high and has relatively large bright yellow flowers that appear in profusion in spring, covering the foliage.

S. spectabile 'Autumn Joy' is one of the finest of the lower-growing stonecrops. It will reach up to 18 inches in height and is hardy in zones 3 to 9. Large light pink flower heads appear in September, gradually turn salmon; by late fall they are coppery red. Flowers then dry on the stem

and remain decorative through the winter. Foliage is light green. 'Meteor' has silver green foliage and showy pink flowers that deepen in color as winter approaches.

S. spurium (sometimes called 'Dragon's Blood') is a creeping, nearly evergreen perennial that forms a 3- to 6-inch mat. Leaves are green and rounded and grow in loose rosettes. Clusters of starry light red flowers bloom in late summer. *S. spurium* is very popular in colder (to -40° F) sections of the country.

Culture Plant stonecrops in sun or light shade, in any type of soil. Water minimally—just enough to keep them healthy and colorful. These plants root easily from cuttings; they even propagate themselves from broken leaves.

Uses Stonecrops are often used as rock garden plants but are also effective on slopes, between stepping-stones, in mass plantings, and as container plants. For an attractive medium-to-large planting, blend them with other ground covers, such as the prostrate junipers (page 82).

Sempervivum
Houseleek

Hardy to zone 5 (-20° F)

Sempervivum tectorum (hen and chickens) is a succulent with fleshy leaves that grow in rosettes. Flowers are star shaped, in tight or loose clusters. Flower color varies: White, yellowish, pink, red, or greenish are common. Many varieties and cultivars with varying heights and flower colors are available.

Culture Hen and chickens is very easy to grow. Plant in sun in well-drained soil. Water only during exceptionally long periods of drought. Propagate by separating offsets.

Uses Planted around rocks, hen and chickens quickly fills in cracks and crevices. It is also a good border plant. On dry slopes it can outgrow and out-compete most weeds.

Skimmia
Skimmia

Hardy to zone 6 (-10° F)

This is a broadleaf evergreen shrub with alternate bright green leaves, up to 5 inches

long, that are fragrant when crushed. Maroon red buds in upright clusters above the leaves open into small and creamy white flowers in spring. Inedible bright red berries may follow. *Skimmia japonica* is densely branched and slow growing to 3 to 5 feet. *S. reevesiana* grows only 18 inches tall, is more compact, and is more useful as a ground cover. Flowers are white; dull crimson red berries appear in fall.

Culture Skimmias do best in shade, in moist, acid soil rich in organic matter, but will withstand filtered sunlight or alkaline soil. Increase by seed or by cuttings taken in fall. Skimmias tolerate urban pollution.

Uses Plant in small, shaded areas, under trees, or in mass shrub plantings. Put them near a patio or path where, when stepped on, fragrance can be enjoyed. Use for edging or as a low hedge. These plants also do well in seaside gardens.

Soleirolia soleirolii (baby's tears)

Spiraea japonica 'Coccinea' (spirea)

Stachys byzantina (lamb's-ears)

Soleirolia
Baby's tears

Hardy to zone 10 (to 32° F)

Soleirolia soleirolii or *Helxine soleirolii* (baby's tears) is a creeping, mosslike plant that forms a dense, soft carpet 1 to 3 inches high. The foliage is composed of tiny, rounded light green leaves that grow in a tight mat.

Culture This plant requires shade, rich soil, and moisture. It is quickly killed by direct sun, drought, or subfreezing temperatures. Propagate by division, planting sections 6 to 12 inches apart. Use outdoors only in the warmest regions.

Uses Baby's tears provides a cool, delicate effect when planted at the base of trees or shade plants such as ferns, camellias, and azaleas. Do not step on the plants; footprints will damage the tender foliage and be visible for days.

Spiraea
Spirea

Hardy to zone 3 (-40° F)

These are tough, trouble-free, fast-growing, deciduous shrubs. Leaves are alternate, mostly toothed; flowers are small and delicate and bloom in showy clusters. *Spiraea × bulmalda* is a mounding shrub that grows from 2 to 3 feet tall and 3 to 5 feet wide with dense, slender branches. White to dark pink flowers in clusters 4 to 6 inches long cover the plant from summer to fall. 'Anthony Waterer' grows 2 to 3 feet tall and has pinkish red flower clusters and maroon-tinged foliage. Sometimes a pink and cream variegation appears on the foliage as it matures. 'Goldflame' has pink blooms and golden yellow foliage. New growth is mottled with red, copper, and orange. Foliage turns crimson in autumn.

S. japonica is hardier than *S. × bumalda* and has a more upright growth habit. *S. j.* 'Alpina' is a low grower (seldom more than 12 inches tall), compact and wide spreading. Pink flower clusters appear in spring. 'Little Princess' grows to 2 feet tall and has rose pink flowers from midsummer to fall. Mint green summer foliage turns red in autumn. 'Shirobana' (or 'Shibori')

grows 2 to 3 feet tall, and has an unusual, simultaneous combination of pink, white, and rose flowers from midsummer into fall. 'Coccinea' is a mounding dwarf (to 3 feet), with crimson flowers from July to August.

Culture Plant spireas in sun or light shade and any but the wettest soil. They are easily transplanted and can be started from cuttings. These plants flower on new growth; prune summer-flowering varieties in late winter or very early spring. Prune spring-flowering types after they finish blooming.

Uses Spireas make good fillers and are also striking in mass plantings. They can be used as accents in the flower garden as well.

Stachys
Lamb's-ears

Hardy to zone 5 (-20° F)

Stachys byzantina (the herb lamb's-ears) got its common name from its shape and woolly softness. It grows to 18 inches high in clumps 3 feet wide. Leaves are 4 inches long

and a silvery gray color that contrasts well with green plants. Purple flowers appear in summer on 1-foot spikes.

Culture Lamb's-ears is easy to grow, requiring only good drainage and full sun. Cut plants back in spring where leaves have been damaged by cold winters. Divide clumps at any time of year.

Uses The gray leaves of lamb's-ears stand out dramatically against the green foliage of other plants. Lamb's-ears also combines well with other gray-foliaged plants, including blue fescue, woolly thyme, and snow-in-summer.

Stephanandra
Stephanandra

Hardy to zone 3 (-40° F)

Stephanandra incisa 'Crispa' is a graceful, mounding, dwarf, deciduous shrub, with delicate, fernlike leaves on arching, slender branches. Leaves are alternate, deeply lobed and toothed, oval to pointed, and up to 2½ inches long. Flowers are small and yellowish white in terminal, 2½-inch panicles, appearing in late spring. This

Stephanandra incisa 'Crispa' (stephanandra)

Taxus baccata 'Repandens' (English yew)

Symphoricarpos albus (snowberry, waxberry)

plant seldom exceeds 2 feet in height but spreads 4 to 5 feet for a fine ground cover.

Culture Stephanandra thrives in shade but may die back in cold winters in the north part of its range. Prune to rejuvenate. Propagate by cuttings, division, or layering. It will root wherever the branches touch the ground.

Uses This plant controls erosion when planted on banks. Use it also in the front of borders or as a low hedge.

Symphoricarpos
Snowberry, coralberry, Indian-currant

Hardy to zone 4 (-30° F)

These hardy, deciduous shrubs are native to much of the United States. Some species grow quite tall, others as low as 3 feet. They spread quickly by underground runners. Flowers of most are not showy but the plants are quite striking when they fruit. Leaves are opposite and rounded, some with a few teeth near the tip. Flowers are small and appear in spring, mostly in small

clusters at the tips or in the leaf axils on red twigs. Fruits are berries borne in pairs or small clusters strung along the stems. They remain on the plant most of the winter.

Symphoricarpos albus (snowberry or waxberry) grows to 4 feet with slender, upright branches that arch slightly. Flowers are pinkish and fruit is white. *S. orbiculatus* (Indian-currant or coralberry) is quite striking in fall when berries and foliage are brilliantly colored. This species grows quickly to 6 feet. 'Leucocarpus' has greenish yellow flowers in summer and white fruits. *S. × chenaultii* (Chenault coralberry) grows 3 to 6 feet tall. Leaves are hairy on the underside; flowers are pinkish; fruit is white—pink on the side exposed to the sun. 'Hancock' (prostrate Chenault coralberry) grows to only 2 feet tall and spreads 6 feet or more. Foliage is bluish green; a heavy crop of rose pink berries appears in September and lasts through November. 'Hancock' and the *S. × doorenbosii* hybrids are the best of this species and deserve further use.

Culture These plants grow in shade but fruit better in sun. They do best in neutral soil but are versatile—as long as their roots receive ample moisture. Prune in spring. Increase by softwood cuttings or divide underground runners.

Uses These are good shrubs for city conditions, useful for holding soil on banks, and for shrub borders in open areas.

Taxus
Yew

Hardy to zone 2 (-50° F)

Low-growing, spreading types of this well-known evergreen conifer can serve as ground covers. Needles are very dark green with lighter undersides. Leaves and bark are toxic. *Taxus baccata* 'Nana' (dwarf English yew) has darker needles and stays about 3 feet high. 'Pygmaea' grows to less than 2 feet tall. 'Repandens' has wide-arching branches with pendulous tips. It grows 2 to 4 feet tall and 12 to 15 feet wide. 'Standishii' is one of the best golden yews for small gardens. *T. baccata* and cultivars are hardy to zone 5.

T. cuspidata is usually grown as a compact, broad-spreading shrub and is hardy in zones 2 to 6. It is scraggly and slow growing and best used only for underplanting in cool, shaded areas. *T. cuspidata* 'Aurescens' grows to 1 to 3 feet. New needles are deep yellow and change gradually to green after the first season. 'Cross Spreading' is highly resistant to winter burn and stays about 3 feet tall. 'Densiformis' grows 3 to 4 feet tall and twice as wide. Needles are bright green.

T. × media 'Chadwickii' is a low spreader with dark green needles that hold color well in winter. 'Everlow' is resistant to wind damage and stays 1½ feet tall. 'Sebian' grows 3 to 4 feet tall and is quite winter hardy and shade tolerant. 'Tauntonii' is one of the best for resisting winter burn and summer heat and does well as far south as zone 8. The other *T. × media* cultivars are all hardy in zones 4 to 7.

Culture Yew grows best in full sun or partial shade in fertile, moist, well-drained,

Teucrium chamaedrys (dwarf germander)

Thymus serpyllum (creeping thyme, mother-of-thyme)

Tiarella cordifolia (foamflower)

neutral soil. Most varieties can be damaged by winter sun and wind. Propagate from cuttings.

Uses   Plant on banks, as hedges, in foundation plantings, and in masses.

Teucrium
Germander

Hardy to zone 3 (-35° F)

Teucrium chamaedrys (dwarf germander) is an undramatic but neat, tough little plant. Stems 6 to 8 inches high are closely covered over their full length by small, serrated medium-green leaves that form a thick cover. Tiny rosy lavender blossoms appear in summer. Growth is rapid by spreading, underground root stems.

Culture   This plant grows in any well-drained soil and does best in full sun. It is a drought-tolerant, heat-loving plant that requires only occasional summer watering. In colder regions, it dies back in winter. Propagate by division or cuttings; set plants 12 to 15 inches apart.

Uses   Dwarf germander is effective in large, informal areas and in desert and rock gardens, where its deep roots bind sandy soil. Shear it to create a low, formal hedge or border.

Thymus
Thyme

Hardy to zone 3 (-40° F)

Several varieties of this herb are commonly used as ground covers. They are prostrate or creeping, have tiny leaves opposite one another that are sometimes covered with delicate white hairs, and produce small flowers on upright spikes. They are, above all, aromatic, releasing their delightful fragrance whenever they are rubbed or walked on.

Thymus serpyllum (creeping thyme, or mother-of-thyme) forms a flat green mat. Upright stems, 3 to 6 inches high, are loosely covered with whorls of tiny pale lavender flowers that appear from late spring through summer. *T. s.* 'Albus' (white creeping thyme) forms a denser, lower mat covered in spring and

summer by a profusion of tiny white flowers. *T. s.* 'Roseus' has pink flowers. *T. ×citriodorus* (lemon thyme) is similar to *T. serpyllum* but has lemon-scented foliage.

T. pseudolanuginosus or *T. lanuginosus* (woolly thyme) has tiny, soft, woolly gray-green leaves that form a dense carpet 2 to 3 inches high. This species tolerates somewhat more traffic than the others. *T. vulgaris* (common thyme) grows to 6 to 12 inches high and is used as a low border for small gardens. *T. v.* 'Argenteus' (silver thyme) has leaves variegated with silver.

Culture   Thymes grow in almost any well-drained soil and do best in full sun but can take some shade. Water regularly in hot-summer areas. Trim periodically. Propagate by division or cuttings taken in spring; set new plants 6 to 12 inches apart.

Uses   Creeping thyme is excellent as a border, in a rock garden, and also on dry slopes. It takes light traffic. White creeping thyme is useful

between stepping-stones. Woolly thyme is strikingly effective between stepping-stones, spilling over a boulder or low bank, or simply alone as a small accent plant.

Tiarella
Foamflower

Hardy to zone 4 (-30° F)

Tiarella cordifolia (foamflower) is an attractive, evergreen to deciduous perennial that makes an excellent ground cover in moist, shady areas. It is native to the woodlands of eastern Canada and the United States and is a close relative of coralbells (*Heuchera*, page 79). The plant's lobed leaves are 2 to 4 inches in diameter. Beautiful, fluffy clusters of white or creamy flowers on 12-inch-high stalks cover the plant in May. The plant spreads vigorously by underground runners.

Culture   This plant grows best in a moist, humus-rich, slightly acid soil. Divide clumps every 2 to 3 years. Propagate by root division in spring or fall.

Trachelospermum asiaticum (Asiatic jasmine)

Vaccinium augustifolium (lowbush blueberry)

Vancouveria hexandra (American barrenwort)

Uses Foamflower makes a fine ground cover in shaded rock gardens, naturalistic areas, and in small, shady niches around the garden.

Trachelospermum
Jasmine

Hardy to zone 7 (0° F)

Trachelospermum jasminoides (starjasmine) is a twining rambler with long, woody stems; handsome, oval deep green leaves; and small, sweetly fragrant, starlike flowers that appear from early spring through summer. Its leaves are 2 to 3 inches long, and its flowers ¾ inch in diameter.

The leaves of *T. asiaticum* (Asiatic jasmine) are smaller and the flowers yellower than those of starjasmine. The alternate facing of the leaves, spaced about 1½ inches apart on the stems, adds to the beauty of the foliage. Both plants are slow to get started and slow growing, but they are quite sturdy once established. Average height is about 1 foot.

Culture These jasmines require shade in desert areas and sun or partial shade elsewhere. They grow best in fairly rich soil and need regular watering throughout the year. Watch for iron chlorosis. Propagate by cuttings; set rooted plants 2 feet apart in spring. Cut back upright shoots. Weed regularly until plants fill in.

Uses These plants are best used in small areas, such as under trees. They can also serve as landscape accents and do well in raised beds.

Vaccinium
Blueberry, mountain cranberry, huckleberry

Hardy to zone 3 (-40° F)

Vaccinium augustifolium (lowbush blueberry) is a straggly, deciduous shrub that grows 1 to 2 feet tall. Leaves are small, alternate, and narrowly elliptic. They are lustrous dark to blue-green in summer and turn brilliant scarlet in fall. Flowers are tiny and urn shaped, white lined

with red, and appear in spring. Edible fruits are blue-black with a white bloom and very sweet. These plants do best in dry, poor, acid soil. (The state of Maine is famous for them.) They are hardy to zone 3 (-40° F). *V. a.* var. *laevifolium* has larger leaves and grows in the southern states.

Vaccinium vitis-idaea var. *minus* (mountain cranberry) is native to the northern United States and Canada. Its range extends from Alaska to Massachusetts, and it is hardy to -30° F. Leaves are about ½ inch long, evergreen, and glossy. Flowers are white to red, bell shaped, and about ¼ inch long. Mountain cranberry spreads by underground runners and makes a dense, even mat 8 inches or less in height. Sour red berries are useful for preserves and syrups.

Culture Plant in moist, acid soil, in partial shade. In mountainous, cool-summer regions, full sun is tolerated, but water plants generously. Propagate by dividing the creeping roots or by transplanting sodlike clumps. Low-

bush blueberry is more resistant to heat and drought. Prune for compact growth.

Uses These plants are most useful in naturalistic gardens, where they can become a floor for shrubs such as large-growing rhododendrons. A single plant in a garden will spread to form a small mat.

Vancouveria
American barrenwort

Hardy to zone 4 (-25° F)

Vancouveria hexandra (American barrenwort) is a Pacific Northwest native closely related to the epimediums (page 71). It grows to 1 to 1½ feet tall. Half-inch white flowers appear in May through June. The leaves are light green and delicate; they die to the ground each winter.

Culture American barrenwort grows naturally in the shade of Pacific Coast redwoods. There, the plant's needs are well met: The soil is acidic and high in organic matter, temperatures are cool, and there is plenty of moisture.

Verbena tenera 'Sissinghurst' (verbena)

Verbena rigida (vervain)

Veronica 'Crater Lake Blue' (speedwell)

Uses This is an excellent ground cover plant where it is well adapted. Combine with ferns and epimediums around the base of trees and in shaded beds.

Verbena
Verbena

Hardy to zone 5 (-20° F)

Spectacular flower colors, a long season of bloom, and a rapid growth rate characterize verbena. *Verbena peruviana* (Peruvian verbena) is a popular evergreen perennial in the Southwest (zones 9 and 10). It grows 4 to 6 inches tall and spreads to form a dense, flat, weed-free mat of small dark green leaves closely spaced along the stems. Brilliant red flowers rise above the foliage in flat-topped clusters and bloom almost continuously from spring through fall.

Among the best cultivars are 'Appleblossom', with light pink flowers 8 to 12 inches high, and 'Little Pinkie', with bright rose pink flowers that bloom late into fall. 'Princess Gloria' has salmon-colored flowers. 'Raspberry Rose' is

a vigorous grower with large dark green leaves. 'Starfire' has bright red flowers and blooms in winter in southern California. These can be grown as annuals in cold-winter areas and as short-lived perennials where winters are warmer.

V. canadensis (rose verbena) grows 18 inches tall and thrives throughout the Southwest and in Mexico. It has pink and purple blooms and is hardy in zones 6 to 10. *V. rigida* (vervain) grows 12 to 18 inches tall and has narrow, sharply toothed leaves 2 to 3 inches long. Purple flowers in open clusters bloom the first year from seed. 'Flame' grows to only 4 inches tall and makes a brilliant carpet. *V. rigida* and cultivars are hardy in zones 7 to 10.

V. tenera 'Sissinghurst' has vibrant rose pink flowers that almost cover the foliage from early summer until frost. This plant is heat and drought tolerant and does very well in the Southeast, spreading up to 4 feet in one summer. With good winter protection in its northern ranges, *V. t.* 'Sissinghurst' is hardy to zone 5. *V.* ✕

hybrida 'Abbeville' has low-growing dark green foliage with delicately fragrant, large terminal clusters of pale lavender blooms from May until frost. It is hardy from zones 5 to 9 with some winter protection.

Culture Verbenas require hot, sunny locations to thrive and produce the most flowers. Once established, they are quite drought tolerant. Water them only infrequently (but deeply) to avoid problems with mildew and other fungal diseases. Cut back perennial plants severely in late fall. Apply a balanced fertilizer after pruning. Propagate with root cuttings planted on 2-foot centers. Verbenas are susceptible to red spider mite and white-fly infestations, especially in the southeastern United States. Control with appropriate insecticides or insecticidal soap.

Uses Verbenas are effective anywhere in the landscape, but especially on sunny, moderate slopes for erosion control. Mix them with phlox, summer-blooming bulbs, or white crinum lilies (*Crinum*) in the flower garden.

Veronica
Speedwell

Hardy to zone 3 (-40° F)

The speedwells are classic garden accent and border plants. The species listed here are evergreen perennials (in most of the United States), with notched, oval to lance-shaped shiny green leaves and attractive flowers, mostly on spikes, that appear in summer. They are vigorous, fast growers that can serve as a lawn substitute, but they do not take traffic. *Veronica incana* (woolly speedwell) forms a tight, 6-inch, gray-green mat with pale blue flowers on long spikes. This species is hardy to -40° F. *V. prostrata* (Hungarian speedwell) has a similar growth habit but spreads more widely and has dark green foliage. It is hardy to 0° F. *V. repens* (creeping speedwell), the lowest-growing variety, forms a 4-inch dark green mat dotted in spring and early summer with clusters of small blue flowers. This makes an excellent lawn substitute and is hardy to -10° F.

Culture These plants grow in full sun or partial shade.

Vinca major 'Pubescens' (periwinkle)

Vinca minor 'Bowles' (dwarf periwinkle)

Viola odorata (violet)

They need good soil and regular watering throughout the growing season. They are easily propagated by division.

Uses Use them alongside paved areas, particularly in shady spots. They can soften the edges of steps or pavement and serve as bulb covers.

Vinca
Periwinkle

Hardy to zone 4 (-30° F)

In form, structure, and growth habit, the periwinkles (*Vinca major* and *V. minor*) are similar. *V. major* is coarser, grows 3 to 4 times as high, is strongly invasive, and is less hardy. Both periwinkles are evergreen trailers: They spread rapidly, with the stems rooting as they trail. Leaves are glossy dark green, growing opposite one another about every inch or so along the stems. In spring, lilac blue flowers appear in moderate numbers toward the stem ends.

V. major grows vigorously to 12 to 18 inches. *V. m.* 'Variegata' ('Elegantissima') has heart-shaped leaves blotched and edged irregularly with creamy white markings. 'Aureomaculata' has a yellow-green blotch in the center of each leaf. 'Jason Hill' has flowers of deeper violet blue.

V. minor (dwarf periwinkle) grows to about 6 inches. The most popular cultivars are 'Alba', 'Miss Jekyll', and 'La Grave'. Of the less common cultivars, 'Albo-variegata' has white flowers and foliage edged with light yellow. 'Argenteo-variegata' has blue flowers and shorter, broader leaves with white margins. 'Azurea Flore Pleno' has sky blue double flowers. The flowers of 'Bowles White' are pink in the bud, white as they open, and quite large. 'Green Carpet' is a nonblooming form with rich green leaves. 'Multiplex' has plum purple double flowers.

Culture Periwinkles grow best in light shade and a good, moist, well-drained soil. Propagate by division or from stem or root cuttings. Set divisions or rooted cuttings 12 inches apart in spring. *V. minor* grows well in any climate in the United States and southern Canada, with the exception of hot desert areas. There, it will grow in the shade but tends to turn yellow, even if watered. *V. minor* is hardy to -30° F. *V. major* is less hardy, tolerating temperatures to -10° F. Several fungal diseases—blight, canker and dieback, leaf spots, and root rot—can be serious problems. Shoots turn dark brown, wilt, and die back to the ground. Provide good air circulation and do not overwater.

Uses *V. minor* is among the best of the evergreen ground covers, not only because of its hardiness but also because of its quiet, cool beauty. It is an excellent choice for medium-scale planting, particularly in the filtered shade of large trees or shrubs. It is also effective in raised beds or planters where it might be designed to trail for several feet. *V. major* is useful as a large-scale ground cover on slopes, particularly in naturalistic gardens and around country homes. Leaves falling from overhead trees vanish beneath its foliage.

Viola
Violet

Hardy to zone 3 (-40° F)

Pansies, violas, and violets are herbaceous perennials belonging to the genus *Viola*. Pansies and violas are commonly grown as annuals or biennials. A few species of violets are useful ground covers. They are 3- to 6-inch-high plants with bright green leaves and ¾-inch-wide spring-blooming flowers in a wide range of solid and mixed colors. They grow in tufts and spread by creeping runners. *V. hederacea* (Australian violet) forms a tight, leafy carpet heavily dotted in summer with typical violet flowers—mostly blue in the center and fading to white at the tips.

V. odorata, the classic violet, has dark green leaves and mostly fragrant flowers. Numerous cultivars are available, with flowers of different sizes and colors. 'Royal Robe' has large deep blue flowers. 'Marie Louise' has fragrant, double white and lavender flowers. 'Royal Elk' has long-stemmed,

Waldsteinia fragarioides (barren strawberry)

Xanthorhiza simplicissima (yellow-root)

Zoysia tenuifolia (Koreangrass)

single, fragrant violet flowers. 'Charm' has small white flowers. 'Rosina' has pink flowers. *V. sororia* is stemless and has large leaves up to 5 inches wide and flat, pansylike whitish flowers with violet blue veins.

Culture To look their best, violets need partial shade, plenty of water, and rich, moist soil. They can be propagated by seed or, faster, by division. Violets produce copious seeds and will naturalize and spread where they are adapted. *V. odorata* and *V. sororia* are hardy to zone 3; *V. hederacea* is much less hardy (to zone 8).

Uses These plants are best for small-scale plantings—as borders, in beds, or around large-leaved evergreen shrubs.

Waldsteinia
Barren strawberry

Hardy to zone 5 (-20° F)

Waldsteinia fragarioides (barren strawberry) is for those who admire the foliage

of the strawberry but do not want the fruit. Like *Duchesnea indica* (page 71), it has 3-leaflet, evergreen leaves, up to 2 inches long, that are toothed at the tips; 5-petaled yellow flowers; and a creeping growth habit. It forms a thick mat 4 to 10 inches high in sun or shade. *W. ternata* is best adapted to southern Canada and the northern United States. In both sunny and shaded locations, it maintains a compact, even, 4-inch height. Leaves are evergreen to semi-evergreen and glossy green in color. Leaflets are smaller than those of *W. fragarioides*—about ½ to 1¼ inches in length.

Culture These plants do best when provided with ample water in well-drained soil. They do not tolerate drought or extended periods of heat. Propagate by seed or division; plant on 12-inch centers.

Uses These plants are too frequently overlooked. Use them on banks, in rock gardens, and around homes.

Xanthorhiza
Yellow-root

Hardy to zone 4 (-30° F)

Xanthorhiza simplicissima (yellow-root) is an easily grown, deciduous shrub. It grows very uniformly to a 2-foot height. Toothed or lobed leaves are 1 to 3 inches long and turn a beautiful yellow-orange in fall. Drooping clusters of tiny purplish flowers appear in May, before the leaves unfold. Spreading roots and stems have an attractive yellow bark.

Culture Yellow-root is tolerant of many soils but grows most luxuriantly in moist soil. It does best in medium to heavy shade. To propagate, dig clumps or take root cuttings.

Uses This is a good plant for low, wet spots—areas for which the choice of plants is limited.

Zoysia
Koreangrass, Mascarenegrass

Hardy to zone 9 (20° F)

Although a true grass, *Zoysia tenuifolia* (Koreangrass) is suitable for use as a ground

cover but not as a turf grass. Its tufting, mounding growth habit creates a lumpy surface practically impossible—and aesthetically undesirable—to mow. It forms a velvety lawn composed of fine, closely growing dark green leaves 3 to 5 inches long. The turf is evergreen wherever temperatures remain above freezing, but it turns brown at the first frost, slowly recovering as temperatures rise. Koreangrass is slow to become established and spread.

Culture This plant does best in well-drained soil, thrives in sun but tolerates light shade. It is drought resistant and needs only moderate watering. New plants are best started by separating sections of root systems and planting them no more than 6 inches apart.

Uses Koreangrass can be used as a lawn substitute in warm climates and where a tailored effect is not desired. It is perhaps most effective in small patio settings, growing between stepping-stones or railroad ties, or on a slope. It accepts light traffic.

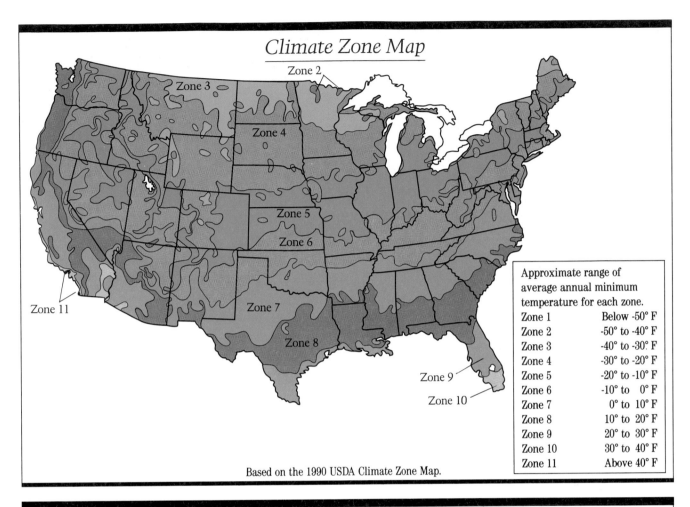

Climate Zone Map

Zone 2
Zone 3
Zone 4
Zone 5
Zone 6
Zone 7
Zone 8
Zone 9
Zone 10
Zone 11

Approximate range of
average annual minimum
temperature for each zone.

Zone 1	Below -50° F
Zone 2	-50° to -40° F
Zone 3	-40° to -30° F
Zone 4	-30° to -20° F
Zone 5	-20° to -10° F
Zone 6	-10° to 0° F
Zone 7	0° to 10° F
Zone 8	10° to 20° F
Zone 9	20° to 30° F
Zone 10	30° to 40° F
Zone 11	Above 40° F

Based on the 1990 USDA Climate Zone Map.

U.S. Measure and Metric Measure Conversion Chart

		Formulas for Exact Measures			Rounded Measures for Quick Reference		
	Symbol	When you know:	Multiply by:	To find:			
Mass	oz	ounces	28.35	grams	1 oz		= 30 g
(Weight)	lb	pounds	0.45	kilograms	4 oz		= 115 g
	g	grams	0.035	ounces	8 oz		= 225 g
	kg	kilograms	2.2	pounds	16 oz	= 1 lb	= 450 g
					32 oz	= 2 lb	= 900 g
					36 oz	= 2¼ lb	= 1000 g (1 kg)
Volume	pt	pints	0.47	liters	1 c	= 8 oz	= 250 ml
	qt	quarts	0.95	liters	2 c (1 pt)	= 16 oz	= 500 ml
	gal	gallons	3.785	liters	4 c (1 qt)	= 32 oz	= 1 liter
	ml	milliliters	0.034	fluid ounces	4 qt (1 gal)	= 128 oz	= 3¾ liter
Length	in.	inches	2.54	centimeters	⅜ in.	= 1 cm	
	ft	feet	30.48	centimeters	1 in.	= 2.5 cm	
	yd	yards	0.9144	meters	2 in.	= 5 cm	
	mi	miles	1.609	kilometers	2½ in.	= 6.5 cm	
	km	kilometers	0.621	miles	12 in. (1 ft)	= 30 cm	
	m	meters	1.094	yards	1 yd	= 90 cm	
	cm	centimeters	0.39	inches	100 ft	= 30 m	
					1 mi	= 1.6 km	
Temperature	° F	Fahrenheit	⅝ (after subtracting 32)	Celsius	32° F	= 0° C	
	° C	Celsius	⅝ (then add 32)	Fahrenheit	212° F	= 100° C	
Area	in.²	square inches	6.452	square centimeters	1 in.²	= 6.5 cm²	
	ft²	square feet	929.0	square centimeters	1 ft²	= 930 cm²	
	yd²	square yards	8361.0	square centimeters	1 yd²	= 8360 cm²	
	a.	acres	0.4047	hectares	1 a.	= 4050 m²	